Contents

Map of the book

Unit	Topics	Listening	Speaking
1 Foundation unit	The CAE exam	All the strategies tested in the exam (see *To the teacher*)	All the strategies tested in the exam (see *To the teacher*)
2 Different backgrounds	Native and adopted countries; comparing different lifestyles	**Strategies:** note-taking; listening for main ideas **Exam questions:** ticking appropriate pictures; answering multiple choice questions	**Strategies:** introducing and talking about yourself or another person; discussing lifestyles; turn-taking **Exam question:** introducing and talking about yourself or another person
3 Unusual homes	Describing and comparing homes	**Strategies:** predicting; listening for main ideas **Exam question:** completing sentences	**Strategies:** coping with vocabulary problems; ranking and reaching agreement **Exam question:** describing and comparing pictures
4 Communicating	Different modes of communication; body language	**Strategies:** interpreting context; listening for main ideas **Exam questions:** identifying pictures; matching extracts with situations; matching extracts with aims	**Strategies:** exchanging views and reporting decisions; ranking and reaching agreement **Exam question:** matching modes of communication and situations
5 Unusual occupations	Work; different jobs	**Strategies:** recognising stress on important words for meaning; listening for main ideas; listening for detail **Exam question:** completing sentences	**Strategies:** role playing; describing and commenting on a photo **Exam question:** describing and identifying two pictures in a series
6 Food and eating habits	Food; restaurants; healthy menus	**Strategies:** inferring attitude; listening for specific information **Exam question:** completing a chart	**Strategies:** using paraphrase; comparing and problem solving **Exam question:** describing and commenting on pictures
7 Expressing your opinions	Opinion surveys and questionnaires; discussion topics; protesting	**Strategies:** listening for specific information; inferring attitude **Exam question:** matching extracts with topics; matching extracts with speakers' reactions	**Strategies:** asking for explanations and clarification; reporting discussions; ranking and reaching agreement **Exam question:** commenting on a photo; discussing purpose

CAMBRIDGE
EXAMINATIONS
PUBLISHING

CAE
Listening and Speaking Skills

Diana Pye and Simon Greenall

CAMBRIDGE
UNIVERSITY PRESS

PUBLISHED BY THE PRESS SYNDICATE OF THE UNIVERSITY OF CAMBRIDGE
The Pitt Building, Trumpington Street, Cambridge, United Kingdom

CAMBRIDGE UNIVERSITY PRESS
The Edinburgh Building, Cambridge CB2 2RU, UK
40 West 20th Street, New York, NY 10011–4211, USA
477 Williamstown Road, Port Melbourne, VIC 3207, Australia
Ruiz de Alarcón 13, 28014 Madrid, Spain
Dock House, The Waterfront, Cape Town 8001, South Africa

http://www.cambridge.org

First published 1996
Reprinted 2003

Printed in the United Kingdom at the University Press, Cambridge

Library of Congress catalog card number

A catalogue record for this book is available from the British Library

ISBN 0 521 48533 9 Student's Book
ISBN 0 521 48534 7 Set of 2 cassettes

Unit	Topics	Listening	Speaking
8 Leadership	Famous leaders; characteristics of leaders	**Strategies:** listening for detail; understanding text organisation; listening for main ideas **Exam question:** matching extracts with people; matching extracts with leadership qualities	**Strategies:** comparing and explaining answers to a questionnaire; expressing and justifying opinions; reaching agreement **Exam question:** discussing statements; reporting and justifying opinions
9 Environmental hazards	Oil tanker disasters; energy sources; dangerous installations	**Strategies:** listening for specific information; inferring and interpreting attitude **Exam question:** matching extracts with people; matching extracts with topics	**Strategies:** expressing and justifying opinions; listening and responding to counter arguments; agreeing and disagreeing **Exam question:** ranking environmental hazards; reaching agreement
10 Conscription	Comparing national service in different countries; different types of national service	**Strategies:** listening for specific information; listening for detail; interpreting context **Exam question:** completing a chart	**Strategies:** discussing arguments for and against a controversial issue; comparing opinions **Exam question:** discussing statements; reaching agreement
11 Time matters	Time and the human body; time management	**Strategies:** listening for main ideas; inferring and interpreting attitude **Exam question:** answering multiple choice questions	**Strategies:** matching cartoons with captions; discussing and drawing conclusions **Exam question:** matching two parts of a sentence; reaching agreement
12 Town and country	Attractive towns and regions; tourist attractions; city life	**Strategies:** listening for specific information **Exam question:** completing a chart; labelling a map	**Strategies:** ranking features of a town; expressing opinions; commenting on a description of a city **Exam question:** describing and drawing a picture

Acknowledgements

We would like to thank:
Our editor Liz Driscoll, for her advice and care over this book.
Lindsay White, Jeanne McCarten, Liz Sharman, Joanne Currie, Randell Harris, Nick
Newton and everybody at Cambridge University Press for making this book possible.

The authors and publishers would like to thank the teachers and students who trialled the
material and whose feedback was invaluable.

The authors and publishers are grateful to the authors, publishers and others who have
given permission for the use of copyright material identified in the text. It has not been
possible to identify the sources of all the material used and in such cases the publishers
would welcome information from copyright owners.

The European for the text 'Serving time over a matter of conscience' on p. 67; Kogan
Page Publishers for the list on p. 76 from 'Managing Your Time' by Lothar J. Seiwert,
Kogan Page Ltd, 1989; *The Observer* for the text on p.78 from 'The Cotswolds'; *The
Independent* for the text on p. 82 from 'America's utopias in the sun' by Geoff
Nicholson.

For permission to reproduce photographs:
Edifice (p. 23 tl, tc, p. 39 mr, bl, p. 85); The Hulton Getty Picture Collection Ltd (p. 16,
p. 52 tl, mr, bl); The Image Bank (p. 19 r, p. 29 mc, br, p. 89 br, p. 90 tr); Images Colour
Library Ltd (p. 29 tc, p. 77, p. 87 mr, p. 88 ml, p. 89 mr, p. 90 ml, p. 92); Millbrook
House Picture Library (p. 20); PA News Ltd/Stefan Rousseau (p. 50); Photofusion Ltd
(p. 29 tr, ml, mr, p. 71 t, p. 89 m, p. 90 tc, p. 93); Pictor International Ltd (p. 23 br,
p. 26, p 71 bc, p. 78 l, p. 89 tr, p. 90 mc, p. 91); Popperfoto (p. 29 bl, p. 52 tl, br);
Powerstock (p. 19 l, p. 23 bc, p. 71 br, p. 87 t, br, p. 88 tl, mr, br, p. 89 tl, tc, p. 90 mr,
bl); Rex Features (p. 31 l, c, p. 52 b, p. 65, p. 67, p. 86, p. 87 mc, p. 88 bl); Frank
Spooner Pictures Ltd (p. 52 tr, p. 59, p. 81); Tony Stone Images (p. 37, p. 39 tr, p. 78 r,
p. 87 ml, mr, bl, p. 88 tc, tr, bc, p. 89 mc, p. 90 br, p. 94); TRIP (p. 32 r).

(t = top, m = middle, b = bottom, l = left; c = centre; r = right)

Illustrations by Bill Piggins (pp. 14, 27) and Erik Liebermann (p. 75).

Commissioned photography by Jeremy Pembrey.

Picture research by Mandy Twells.

Layout by Newton Harris.

To the student

About the exam

The Certificate in Advanced English (CAE) is for students at an advanced level of English. To give you an idea of the level, you may have taken the Cambridge First Certificate of English (FCE) and obtained a grade C or above. However, this is not essential if you want to sit the CAE.

There are five papers in the exam: Reading (Paper 1), Writing (Paper 2), English in Use (Paper 3), Listening (Paper 4), and Speaking (Paper 5). This book helps you prepare for Listening (Paper 4) and Speaking (Paper 5). You may like to use *CAE Reading Skills and CAE Writing Skills* to help you prepare for Papers 1 and 2.

Paper 4 (Listening) takes approximately 45 minutes. There are three basic question types: multiple choice, gap fill and matching techniques. The texts come from a number of different sources, such as radio broadcasts and announcements, conversations and discussions, speeches, talks and lectures and interviews with people in the street. There are four sections, A, B, C and D and there will be 40 and 50 questions or items. Sections A, C and D are heard twice; Section B is heard once only. The text type in Section A is usually a monologue, in Section B a short descriptive passage, in Section C a dialogue or discussion and in Section D a series of short extracts lasting about 10–30 seconds. The skills tested are extracting main information, understanding gist or general impressions, the attitudes and points of view of the speakers and identifying the speakers or source or nature of what you are listening to.

It is a good idea to choose your answers carefully and write them on the exam paper, then transfer your answers in pencil to the Answer sheet. You can see an example of the Answer sheet on page 100 of this book. Study the Answer sheet carefully before the exam so that it will not come as a surprise when you take the exam.

Paper 5 (Speaking) takes about 15 minutes; you take it with another candidate. There may be two examiners in the room; one is to conduct the interview and the other is to help in assessing your speaking ability. There are four phases; each one lasts three or four minutes. In Phase A, the examiner will invite you to talk about yourselves and ask questions about your background, interests, career and plans. In Phase B, the examiner will ask you to describe and identify a photo. In Phase C, you will have a problem-solving activity to discuss with the other candidate. In Phase D, the examiner will invite you to report back on your discussion in Phase C and develop it.

The Speaking Paper is marked according to five criteria: fluency, accuracy, pronunciation, task achievement and interactive communication.

About this book

This book is designed to give you practice in developing the different listening and speaking skills which are tested in the exam, and in answering the exam questions themselves. You need to be very familiar with the exam question types in order to answer them effectively.

You can use this book in class, alone or with a partner, or as self-study material working at home. The answers are at the back of the book, but try not to look at them before you have tried to answer the questions on your own.

There is a progression of difficulty in the material but you can dip into different units in any order you like. There are two sections in each unit, each taking about 60 minutes. Section A is concerned with listening; Section B focuses on speaking. In each section there are exam tips and study tips to help you. Unit 1 provides you with a great deal of information about the exam which we hope you will find useful.

We have chosen topics which we hope you will enjoy listening to and speaking about. Your motivation is extremely important in your preparation for the exam, and we have tried to provide texts and tasks which will interest you.

Good luck with *CAE Listening and Speaking Skills*, and good luck with the exam!

Diana Pye   Simon Greenall

To the teacher

Aims

CAE Listening and Speaking Skills aims to help you prepare your candidates for Paper 4 (Listening) and Paper 5 (Speaking) of the Certificate in Advanced English (CAE). Our principal aim is to provide systematic coverage of the specific skills needed for the two papers of the exam. However, in keeping with the declared spirit of the exam, which is designed to reflect current developments in methodology and teaching practice, as well as to test students' language competence, our secondary aim is to provide a thorough presentation and development of the various skills needed for effective listening comprehension and speaking ability at an advanced level.

The book contains a great deal of information about the exam itself, and in particular, about the exam question types, about the strategies required to answer the questions successfully, and about the texts used.

You can use the book as a self-study book, either in the classroom or for students working at home. It can also be used interactively in the classroom if you require extra material to supplement the main course of preparation for the exam. Although we have chosen topics and text types which reflect those you would expect to find in the exam, we have also selected them with the interests and motivation of the non-examination class in mind. Even if you find yourself with a class in which some students have not yet decided to take the exam, you will be able to use the book for advanced level listening and speaking skills.

Organisation

The book is divided into twelve units.

The Foundation unit (Unit 1) uses a 'loop' format in which information about the exam is presented using activities similar to the question types in the exam. Helping the candidates become familiar with the exam format is an important part of your exam preparation class; we hope that you will find this approach useful and challenging.

Each of the remaining eleven units is divided into two sections, the first on listening and the second on speaking. The two sections are thematically linked.

In Section A of each unit you will find:
– one or more exam-type listening texts.
– a series of activities to contextualise the texts and activities and to prepare the candidates for listening.

– an activity or two which prepare the candidates specifically for a particular exam question type.
– a specific exam question type.
– an exam tip box, containing advice specific to the question type under scrutiny in the section.
– follow-up activities and discussion work.

In Section B of each unit you will find:
– one or more exam-type speaking tasks, linked thematically to those in the preceding section.
– a series of activities contextualising the passages designed to develop the candidates' speaking strategies in a way that is relevant to their level.
– an exam tip box, containing advice on how to develop speaking strategies, and information about the exam.
– follow-up activities and discussion work.

Each section will take about 60 minutes to teach but you may find that the topics selected and material provided are rich enough to extend discussion beyond this time limit if students' interest is sustained.

Listening and speaking skills

The following Listening skills are systematically covered:
– understanding and sequencing main ideas
– listening for specific information
– interpreting attitude, point of view
– identifying and interpreting context, topic, function, information

In order to develop these skills a number of strategies are focused on and practised. These include predicting, stress timing, recognition of discourse markers, recognition of repetition and rephrasing, dealing with unfamiliar vocabulary.

In the Speaking sections, the activities are designed to provide students with the opportunity to develop and practise the target skills of the different phases of the CAE Speaking exam, which are:
– general interactional and social language
– transactional language
– negotiation and collaboration skills
– reporting, explaining, summarising, developing the discussion

Suggestions for use

It was mentioned earlier that the book can be used for self-study or interactively in the classroom. As self-study material, it can be used for home study or in the classroom. Encourage your students to choose the units which interest them, or direct them to units which provide practice in areas in which you consider they could benefit from some improvement. During a later lesson, it is a good idea to find out how successfully they have worked alone by checking if they have answered the questions correctly.

As classroom material, you may also want to leave out certain units and activities or spend more time on some than on others. You can let students work alone, in pairs or in groups. All the activities can be used for discussion practice even though this is not specified in the instructions.

There is a progression in the difficulty of the material so that you can use it as an extended course of systematic training for the exam. But it is also expected that you may want to dip into it in a random way, using it as a resource to supplement your existing main course of training. Both approaches are equally appropriate.

The exam tips are placed either before or after the exam question they refer to. Sometimes it may be better to let students read the tips before they answer the question. On other occasions, you may want to let them do the activity and then read the advice. They can then do the activity again, with the advice in mind, to see if they are more successful.

When you come to an exam tip box, here are some suggestions on classroom procedure:
– ask students to read the information to themselves.
– ask them to summarise the information from memory with a partner.
– find out if anyone believes that they already use the strategies suggested, or were aware of the information the box contained.
– find out if students can remember what the preceding exam tip box contained, and if the advice is relevant to anything they have done in the present section.
– ask them to do, or redo, the questions to which the advice refers.
– ask them to decide if the information is useful.

Some of the boxes contain similar information. This is a deliberate attempt to recycle and revise the tips in a systematic way.

Above all, the book was written with pleasure, and is intended to be used with pleasure, with special emphasis on the flexibility of use. We hope you enjoy using *CAE Listening and Speaking Skills*.

Diana Pye   Simon Greenall

UNIT

1

Foundation unit

Section A Listening

1 You are going to hear a recording in which an organiser of the CAE exam is describing the Listening Paper to a group of people.

🔲 🔑 Listen to the recording. Who do you think the people listening to the presentation are?

candidates for the exam   future examiners   teachers

What helped you make up your mind? Be prepared to explain your reasons to the class.

2 Look at the list of sub-topics below. They are all mentioned in the presentation of the CAE Listening Paper in activity 1.

> number of times each text is heard   length of exam
> number of items   text types   question types   text sources
> number of sections   skills tested   instructions

Work in pairs. What sort of information would you expect to hear for each sub-topic?

⌗0 Listen to the recording from activity 1 again. Number the sub-topics in the order in which they are mentioned.

With your partner, discuss the information you heard for each sub-topic.

TIP

We often listen in order to retrieve specific pieces of information which are particularly relevant to us. In this respect, listening is a process of selection in which it is not necessary to understand every word. You should listen for words or expressions which are related to the information you are interested in and concentrate on that particular part of the speech, interview, announcement etc. Here again, recognition of key words can help you listen for the important points without worrying about understanding every word.

---

3 The chart below is adapted from the section of the CAE Specifications leaflet on the Listening Paper. What sort of information would you expect to find in the chart?

Listening	Text type	Number of times text is heard	Text length
Section A			
Section B			
Section C			
Section D			

⌗0 Listen to the recording from activity 1 again. Complete the chart. You will not hear the information needed to complete three of the blanks.

TIP

When we listen to our own language, we register and interpret many details about the situation and the speakers involved without being consciously aware of what we are doing. However, when we listen to a foreign language, we may have difficulty processing many of the background details, such as accent, tone, register, function and attitude of the speakers.

---

4 You are going to hear five short extracts. They are not related in any way except that four of them deal with the same general topic.

🔲 ⏻ Listen to the recording. What is the general topic? Which four extracts deal with it?

Do any of the speakers have noticeable accents? If so, can you identify their accents?

5 ⏻ Listen to the recording from activity 4 again. Complete the chart below.

Extract	Number of speakers	Setting	Role of speakers	Attitude of speakers
1				
2				
3				
4				
5				

Section B Speaking

1 You are going to hear two candidates taking Phase A of the CAE Speaking Paper.

Read the questions below before you listen to the recording.

1 How many people participate in the conversation? Who are they? Do they know each other? Who speaks the most?
2 How many different topics are covered?
3 Who is responsible for changing topic?
4 How are new topics introduced?
5 How do the speakers take turns? Do they interrupt, do they answer a direct question or do they do this in some other way?
6 Would you say that the two candidates perform equally well? Or is one noticeably better than the other?

Listen to the recording and answer the questions.

Work in pairs. Compare your answers.

2 With your partner, discuss the statements about Phase A of the Speaking Paper below. Decide whether the statements are true or false. Be prepared to explain your answers to the class.

1 It is a good idea to rehearse Phase A thoroughly beforehand.
2 It is important to listen carefully to the other participants.
3 No visuals are used in this phase.
4 Only one examiner participates in the conversation.
5 Grammatical accuracy is essential in this phase.
6 You should speak as much as you can.
7 It is an advantage to take the exam with a candidate you know.

TIP

When you are required to convey information to another person, for example, when describing something or giving instructions, it is important to present your ideas in a clear and orderly way. The listener should be able to recognise a logical progression in the presentation of your ideas. When faced with vocabulary problems, you can use paraphrase and synonyms to get your meaning across. It is important to be sensitive to the listener's reactions, such as looks of puzzlement, surprise or even blank incomprehension, and respond accordingly, for example, by repeating or rephrasing what you have said.

3 ⚏ **Look at the list of activity-types below. Which of these are most likely to help you develop the skill of conveying information? Decide which ones you consider to be most useful. Put them in order from 1 (not very useful) to 8 (very useful).**

a) group discussions
b) listening to recordings of descriptions or stories
c) describing things in detail in your own language
d) performing information gap activities in pairs
e) telling stories in your own language
f) listening to your teacher giving instructions
g) playing games
h) describing pictures

Discuss your answers with your partner.

4 **You are going to hear an extract from Phase B of the Speaking Paper in which Candidate A is describing a photo to Candidate B.**

🖭 ⚏ **Listen to the recording. How would you define Candidate A's description?**

bitty   clear   difficult to follow   muddled   well-organised

How did Candidate B interpret the scene in the photo? Did she include impressions, feelings or opinions?

5 ⚏ **With your partner, discuss what you have learned about Phase B of the Speaking Paper.**

TIP

In many real-life situations, at work, for instance, we may be required to collaborate with other people in order to solve a particular problem. To collaborate successfully, it is important to listen carefully to what other people have to say and to take their opinions into account when reaching a final decision rather than aggressively imposing one's own opinions. Stating clearly one's ideas and explaining them where necessary are also essential elements of a fruitful discussion. It is not always essential to come to a common agreement but sometimes, when a decision has to be taken, a compromise must be reached on the basis of the various opinions.

6 **You are going to hear an extract from Phase C of the CAE Speaking Paper.**

Read the questions below before you listen to the recording.

1 What is the topic of discussion?
2 What conclusions do the candidates come to?
3 Does one candidate speak more than the other?
4 What language do they use to express agreement and disagreement?
5 Whose arguments are the most convincing? Why?

Listen to the recording and answer the questions.

Compare your answers with your partner.

TIP

When you have satisfactorily solved a problem or come to a compromise, it is often necessary to report and justify the conclusion that you have reached. Here again, you should be clear and concise. When an explanation is confused, it is either because the ideas themselves are not sufficiently clear or because the language used does not fully express the ideas. It is therefore preferable to express a few simple ideas using appropriate language rather than trying to convey a number of complex ideas with inadequate language.

7 **Look at the list of language functions below. Think about the three phases of the Speaking Paper. Which of these language functions are you most likely to use in each phase?**

agreeing and disagreeing   comparing and contrasting
describing objects or people   explaining decisions
expressing opinions   greetings   interpreting a picture
introducing yourself or others   justifying opinions   persuading
reporting   summarising   talking about likes and dislikes

Discuss your answers with your partner.

8 ⌐0 The following Assessment criteria are taken into consideration when marking the Speaking Paper. Match the criteria with their explanations.

accuracy   fluency   pronunciation   task achievement
interactive communication

a) participating effectively in conversations and discussions
b) using a wide range of language structures and vocabulary
c) speaking at a natural pace without too many hesitations
d) using intonation and stress patterns correctly
e) carrying out tasks effectively using appropriate language

9 ⌐0 Look at the Assessment grid on page 99. Listen to the recordings from activities 1, 4 and 6 again. Use the information in the grid to assess the candidates' performance. Be prepared to explain your decision to the class.

10 Think about your own speaking ability. Which of the five criteria would you score well on? Which would you score badly on?

Discuss your answers with your partner. Decide which aspects of your speaking you particularly need to improve.

2

Different backgrounds

Section A Listening

The aim of this section is to focus on the following.
- note-taking
- listening for main ideas without being distracted by detail

The first exam question requires you to identify pictures which illustrate information in a recording. The second exam question requires you to answer multiple choice questions.

1 In this unit you are going to hear a number of people who have left their native countries to live abroad. They are talking about their experiences.

Work in pairs. List the various reasons that people may have for going to live in a different country. What problems are they likely to come across?

2 Here are some questions that you could ask someone who has left his or her country to live in a foreign country.

1 Why did you leave your country?
2 How long have you been living in your new home?
3 What do you miss about your native home?
4 What is similar to your native home?
5 What is different?
6 What do you like about your new home?
7 What do you dislike?

Can you think of two or three more questions?

What sort of answers would you expect? Write a few words in answer to each question.

3 ☐☐ ⌐0 Listen to two interviews with people who live away from their native homes. Where do they come from and where do they live now?

Which questions in activity 2 do the two people answer? For each speaker, write down the number of the questions in the order in which they answer them.

Note-taking is a strategy which you will need for many of the tasks in the exam. It is not usually a good idea to rely on your memory alone, especially when you are listening for specific details of information. When you take notes, only write down important words for meaning and specific details such as dates which you are not likely to remember. Do not attempt to write full sentences or what the person actually says; this is likely to distract your attention from the listening task and you will miss information.

4 🎧 **Listen to the recording from activity 3 again and answer the questions from activity 2. Take notes as you listen to the interviews.**

5 **Imagine you are going to live in New York. With your partner, discuss what differences there are likely to be from life in your country. What are the advantages and disadvantages likely to be?**

Exam questions of the type below are often found in Section A of the Listening Paper. The task involves listening for main ideas. In the time you have before the recording is played, look very carefully at the pictures and decide exactly what they show. If you can, describe them to yourself in as much detail as possible. This will help you check if the information they represent is mentioned in the recording.

6 📼 🎧 *Exam Question*   You will hear an interview with Sean Fitzpatrick, an Irishman who went to live in New York. Tick those pictures which show Sean in his new life and put a cross against those which are not mentioned. Listen carefully. You will hear this piece twice.

7 ⚷ *Exam Question*   Because you have already heard the recording in activity 6, read and answer the multiple choice questions based on what you can remember.

Choose the best answer A, B, C or D.

1 Why did he go to America?
    A It was a childhood dream.
    B Because he found a job as a barman.
    C Because he lost his driving licence.
    D Because of the troubles in Ireland.

2 What does he miss from home?
    A The social life.
    B Nothing.
    C Only his family and friends.
    D Football.

1	
2	
3	
4	
5	
6	
7	

3 Why is life in New York more exciting?
    A There are parties every night.
    B People spend more money.
    C There are more things to do.
    D The lifestyle is much faster.

4 What does he like in particular?
    A Gambling.
    B Watching ice hockey matches.
    C The sports.
    D His job.

5 What was his best moment since he came to America?
    A Going to watch the 1990 Superbowl.
    B Going to Los Angeles for the World Cup.
    C Seeing Ireland play in Florida.
    D Going home to see his family.

6 What could be better there?
    A There are no real pubs.
    B People are not very friendly.
    C It's a dangerous place to live.
    D Things are very expensive.

7 Has living in New York changed him?
    A It has made him a bit more tolerant of other people.
    B He is better able to defend himself.
    C He is no different at all.
    D He has calmed down a lot since he's been in New York.

Section B Speaking

The aim of this section is to focus on the following.

- introducing yourself or a friend to a third person
- discussing lifestyles
- focusing on turn-taking in conversation

The exam question prepares you for Phase A of the exam; it requires you to introduce and talk about yourself or about a friend.

1 Work in pairs. Look at the photo above and discuss the questions below.

- Who are these people?
- Where did they come from?
- How do you think they felt?
- What do you think they were looking forward to?
- What do you think their lives were like in their old countries?
- Why did they emigrate?

Can you think of similar situations in the world today? Do people emigrate for similar reasons today?

2 Think of a foreign country which interests or appeals to you. Imagine you are going to live there.

Work in small groups and discuss the questions below.

- What major differences in lifestyle are you likely to find?
- What do you think you would find most difficult to adapt to?
- What do you think you would miss most about home?
- What do you think you would most appreciate about your new home?

Now discuss these questions. Be prepared to explain your answers to the class.

- Is there another country where you would like to live?
- Do you think you will ever live abroad?
- What countries have a lifestyle you think you would find it difficult to adapt to?

3 Make notes about your country. Think about the following.

population   geography   climate   famous landmarks
typical products

This is all information you may be able to use in Phase A of the exam.

4 Work in pairs. What impressions do you think visitors have when they first come to your country? Make a list. Are you proud of the general impression that visitors might have?

5 Work in pairs. Take turns to ask and answer questions about each other's background. Talk about the following.

- where you were born
- where you live now
- where you went to school
- how many brothers and sisters you have
- what you like doing in your free time
- how long you've been learning English
- if you need English for your work

How many similarities and differences are there in your backgrounds?

6 Make a list of any other questions you could ask your partner about his or her background. Think about your own answers to your questions as well.

Take turns to ask and answer your questions.

EXAM TIP

In the interview, you will be examined by two examiners. One is known as the interlocutor, who is the person who will set the tasks and give you the opportunity to show how well you speak. The other is the assessor, who will only join in during Phase D of the interview, but who helps decide on the final marks to give you. In Phase A of the exam, you will have a conversation with another candidate and the examiner. If you don't already know the other candidate, you will probably be asked to find out about him or her. You are expected to ask each other questions about your families, what you do, your interests, why you are learning English, your plans for the future, etc.

The other questions you will be asked depend on whether you are in the UK or in your own country.

Here are some of the questions the examiner may ask you.
Good morning. My name is … and this is … .
What are your names?
We'd like to find out about you. Do you know each other?

If you know each other, the examiner may continue like this:
So, perhaps you can tell us about Candidate B.
Where's he/she from? What does he/she like doing in his/her free time?
And would you like to tell us something about Candidate A, please? How long have you known each other?
What do you know about each other's country?

If you don't know each other, the examiner may continue like this:
Perhaps you can tell each other where you're from, what you do, what you like doing in your free time, and so on.
Why are you studying English? Do you need English for your work?

The aim of this phase is to judge your conversation ability. It is therefore just as important to listen to the other people and respond to them as it is to talk about yourself. Remember, in conversation, everybody should have a chance to speak!

7 *Exam Question* Work in groups of three.

STUDENT A: You are the examiner. Turn to page 84 for your instructions.
STUDENTS B and C: You are exam candidates in the interview. Take turns to ask each other the questions you used in activities 5 and 6.

8 Repeat activity 7 to allow Student A the opportunity to speak.

STUDENT B: You are the examiner. Turn to page 84 for your instructions.
STUDENTS A and C: You are exam candidates in the interview.

9 Try to remember everything you mentioned about yourself in the unit. Make notes. You may be able to use this information in Phase A of the exam itself.

UNIT
3

Unusual homes

Section A Listening

The aim of this section is to focus on the following.

- predicting what a recording is about
- listening for the main ideas of a recording

The exam question prepares you for Section C of the exam; it requires you to complete sentences with information from a recording by writing a word or a short phrase.

1 Work in groups of three. Look at the photos of unusual homes below. Make a list of the possible advantages and disadvantages of living in these homes. What possible reasons do you think people may have for choosing to live in a windmill, a house boat and a railway carriage?

You are more likely to recognise and understand what someone is saying if you already have an idea of the topic, who the speakers are, and the sort of things they will mention.

Before listening to a recording in English, you may find it helpful to think about the topic. You may even wish to note down a few ideas which you think the speakers may mention.

In a listening task in an exam, you can guess quite a lot of information by carefully reading the questions beforehand. This sort of preparation can also help you not to panic in a stressful exam situation.

2 You are going to hear interviews with people who live in these three types of home.

Listen to the recording. Tick any advantages and disadvantages you noted in activity 1 which the speakers mention.

What advantages do the speakers mention which are not on your list? What were the main reasons for their choice of home?

3 In your group, try to answer these questions.

1 What state were the homes in when their owners first bought them?
2 How did the people feel at first?
3 How long have they lived there?
4 What conversions have they made?
5 Where are their homes situated?

Try to remember as much detail as possible. Which questions are not answered?

4 Listen to the recording from activity 2 again. Check your answers to the questions in activity 3. Take turns in your group to summarise what the speakers say.

Compare what the three speakers say with your ideas in activity 1.

5 Are all three speakers satisfied with their homes? Choose the sentence which best sums up the way each person feels.

a) It makes things very complicated, living here.
b) It is much more practical than I had ever imagined.
c) I would still prefer a house with a garden.
d) I love the feeling of space and the fact that you can change the scenery.
e) The beautiful setting makes up for any daily inconvenience.

EXAM TIP

In Section C of the exam, you may be asked to complete sentences with information from a recorded interview. The information is not always stated clearly so you may have to interpret this meaning from what the person actually says.

The questions always follow the order of the interview and usually focus on important points. They only require very short answers which are generally words or expressions used by the speaker.

Make sure you read the sentences very carefully so that you know the sort of information you will be listening for. You may even be able to predict some of the answers. In the exam, you will only hear the recording once. But, because you will hear the recording twice in the exam question below, you can identify the information and write in the more obvious missing words the first time you listen; then write in the other missing words and check them all the second time you listen.

6 🖭 🎧 *Exam Question* You will hear an interview with Peter Mitchell, who lives in a tree house. Look at the sentences and complete them by writing one or two words in the spaces. Listen carefully. You will hear this piece twice.

As a child Peter Mitchell had often dreamt of ⟦1 ⟧ a tree house.

The house is built in a magnificent ⟦2 ⟧.

He used to work as a ⟦3 ⟧.

He started building the tree house when he needed ⟦4 ⟧.

Because it is built of recycled old building materials, the house cost ⟦5 ⟧.

Before moving in permanently he used the tree house as a ⟦6 ⟧.

He particularly appreciates the feeling of belonging to ⟦7 ⟧.

The house has withstood ⟦8 ⟧ without being damaged.

The construction has not ⟦9 ⟧ the tree or restricted ⟦10 ⟧.

He has not had any trouble with the ⟦11 ⟧ because as yet you do not need ⟦12 ⟧ for a tree house.

7 Would you like to live in one of the homes mentioned in this unit? Find out which home other students would choose. Ask them to explain their choice.

Section B Speaking

The aim of this section is to focus on the following.
- coping with vocabulary problems by asking for help or using paraphrase
- ranking characteristics and reaching agreement

The exam question prepares you for Phase B of the exam; it requires you to describe a picture and compare it with the description of a similar picture.

STUDY TIP

One of the most frustrating problems facing a learner is not knowing or not being able to remember a particular word or expression. This type of difficulty also occurs quite frequently in your own language and you get round it by using a number of strategies. These strategies are also likely to be very useful in the foreign language.

- Sometimes there are a number of words which have more or less the same meaning. If you can't think of the exact word, use a synonym or a word with a similar meaning.
- If you don't know the right word or one with a similar meaning, you can use paraphrase or explain your meaning with a complete sentence or description.
- Finally, if you really do need a word or expression, you can always ask another person for help. You can say:

I don't know how to say it.	*What is the English for … ?*
I don't know what you call it.	*What is (own language word) in English?*
I don't know the word in English.	*How do you say (own language word) in English?*
What do you call it?	

1 🔊 Work in pairs. Look at the words and expressions below. Do they have positive or negative meanings? Which words have similar meanings? Underline the stressed syllables and say the words aloud.

> attractive   austere   charming   dangerous   demolish   derelict
> do up   falling down   hideous   improve   property   pull down
> renovate   restore   ruin   run down   severe-looking   solid
> masonry   structurally sound   ugly   unsafe

2 Which of the words and expressions in activity 1 would you use to describe the properties in the photos? What do you think the buildings were originally used for?

3 Discuss these questions with your partner.

- What would have to be done to restore these buildings and to turn them into living accommodation?
- How much do you think it would cost to do this work in your country?
- Is it fashionable in your country to do up old properties or do people generally prefer to build new homes?

4 Work in groups of three or four. Choose one of the properties from the photos. Imagine that your group is responsible for selling the property. What would you say if you were trying to persuade someone to buy it?

Decide which of the following features you consider to be most important. Put them in order from 1 (not very important) to 10 (very important).

- a garage and two outhouses
- plenty of scope for redevelopment
- 15 minutes' drive from an attractive market town
- bargain price
- a charming property in an idyllic setting
- a lot of character
- an excellent long-term investment
- river fishing rights
- a lively neighbourhood
- an interesting property for people with character

Remember to ask the other students in your group for help with words that you do not know.

5 Work with a student from another group. Take turns to try and sell your property to your partner.

A common exam task is Spot the difference. Here is what the examiner is likely to say about two pictures of houses.

Candidate A, look at this picture. Candidate B, look at this one.

The pictures are similar but not the same. Candidate A, describe your picture fully to Candidate B. Talk about the house, the state it is in, what needs doing to it. You have about a minute for this.

Candidate B, listen carefully. Then tell us briefly two things which are the same in your picture and two things which are different. You may ask Candidate A one or two questions if you are uncertain about a detail.

Now compare your pictures.

This type of task is set in Phase B of the CAE exam and is designed to test how good you are at giving information. It is your main opportunity to speak for a sustained period of time, so you must take full advantage of it.

In the question below, you are asked to describe a house and you will therefore have to mention a certain number of details. If you can't remember the exact words for something, use words you know to describe it – the examiner will give you marks if you show you can get round vocabulary problems effectively.

You will have to speak for about a minute, so if you have finished your description before being told to stop, add a few general or even personal comments about your picture.

When you are listening to the other candidate describing his or her picture, you may ask for an explanation or for something to be repeated. If your partner is having difficulty with a detail, you may help by asking a question. Don't forget, you will be given extra marks if you show you are able to respond sensitively to other people.

6 *Exam Question* Work in groups of three.

STUDENT A: Turn to page 85.
STUDENT B: Turn to page 86.
STUDENT C: You are the examiner. Look at both pictures on pages 85 and 86 and listen to Candidates A and B. When they have finished, ask them to compare the pictures. Make suggestions for things they could have mentioned, and comment on the way things were expressed.

7 Work in groups of three or four. Tell the others about your own home. Talk about the features below.

type of home   location   view   number and type of rooms
style of furniture   state of decoration when you moved there
state of decoration now   most attractive features
features you'd most like to change

Are you happy with your homes or would you like to move?

4

Communicating

Section A Listening

The aim of this section is to focus on the following.

- interpreting context: identifying the number, identity and role of speakers, inferring relationships, inferring attitude from tone of voice and type of language used
- listening for main ideas

The first exam question prepares you for Section A of the exam; it requires you to identify pictures which illustrate information in a recording. The second exam question prepares you for Section D of the exam; Task 1 requires you to match extracts with situations; Task 2 requires you to match extracts with aims.

1 Look at the means of communication below. Which ones do you use? Which have you never used? Which have you only used once or twice?

> answerphone   car phone   computer modem   cordless phone   fax
> homing pigeon   intercom unit   letter   loud speaker   messenger
> mobile phone   telegram   telephone

Work in pairs. Compare your answers. Think of situations where each means of communication could be useful.

2 Read the statements below. With your partner, decide what means of communication they are likely to refer to.

a) It's essentially a professional tool, although it does come in handy now and again at home – for booking the annual holiday, that sort of thing.

b) I spend hours chatting to my friends when I get fed up with being stuck at home. It makes my parents really mad.

c) It's the only really civilised way of staying in contact with old friends. It's also a marvellous way of passing the time – which does pass slowly when you're retired, you know.

d) Because I'm confined to a wheelchair, it's an absolute lifeline for me.

e) It saves me running up and down stairs to see if he's still asleep.

Who might make the statements?

Outside the classroom, interpreting context is not very often a problem because you are usually involved in, and not just listening to, the conversation. However, when you listen to recorded materials in the classroom or during an exam, you need to be able to understand the context of the listening extracts. In this respect, interpreting context is essentially a classroom and exam strategy.

Background noise can be helpful for identifying where the speakers are and what the situation is. It is also important to recognise how many people are speaking and who they are. Do the speakers know one another or are they strangers? What is their role and status? The language they use and the tone of voice are clues to the relationships between people. For example, informal language is usually used between friends, more formal, stereotyped language between strangers.

3 You are going to hear five people talking about different means of communication.

Listen to the recording. Match the statements in activity 2 with the speakers. What mode of communication is each speaker talking about?

4 Listen to the recording from activity 3 again. Decide who the speakers are. Choose from the list below.

business person   disabled person   elderly person   holiday maker journalist   parent   policeman   school teacher   shopkeeper teenager

EXAM TIP

When you do the question type in the Exam question below in Section A of the exam, you will have two opportunities to listen and extract the correct information. Make quite sure that you understand what is shown in the pictures. You are usually asked to tick the pictures which are correct and put a cross by the ones which are wrong or not mentioned, but an additional variation may be to number the correct pictures in the order in which you hear the information describing them.

5 *Exam Question* You will hear someone giving foreign visitors to Britain advice on how to make use of the telephone services in Britain. Tick those pictures which show what you should do and put a cross against those which are wrong or are not mentioned. Listen carefully. You will hear this piece twice.

EXAM TIP

The type of question in the Exam question below is common in Section D of the exam. The recording for Section D is heard twice, as for Sections A and C. The speakers may have light accents, such as American or Australian, and there may be some background noise, but this is usually faded out before the text is tested. The first task usually focuses on the type of speaker or the topic; the second task often focuses on the aim or intention of the extract. You will hear extracts from radio broadcasts, speeches, talks, lectures, interviews and conversations. Make sure that you read the situations and aims very carefully.

6 *Exam Question* You will hear various people talking. You will hear the people twice.

Task 1
Look at the situations listed below. As you listen, decide in what order you hear them mentioned and complete the boxes with the appropriate letter. Three situations will not be used.

A a telephone conversation
B the station information desk
C a friendly chat over breakfast
D in a head teacher's office
E asking for directions in the street
F a message on an answerphone
G a radio news bulletin
H in a car

1	
2	
3	
4	
5	

Task 2
Look at the aims listed below. As you listen, put the aims in the order in which you hear them mentioned and complete the boxes with the appropriate letter. Three aims will not be used.

A apologising for something
B enquiring about something
C describing something
D arguing with someone
E giving someone advice
F warning someone
G asking someone to do something
H making a promise

6	
7	
8	
9	
10	

Section B Speaking

The aim of this section is to focus on the following.

– exchanging views and reporting decisions
– ranking and reaching agreement

The exam question prepares you for Phase C of the exam; it requires you to match modes of communication with situations and reach agreement or agree to disagree.

1 Work in pairs. Look at the photos below and describe them. Talk about the following.

– what the situation is
– what the person is saying
– how he or she is saying it
– what his or her feelings are

How can you tell? What gestures and other aspects of body language can help you make up your mind?

2 Here are some more questions about communicating without words. Read and answer the questions.

---

1 How close do you stand or sit to someone when you speak to them?

2 Do you look people in the eye when you speak to them? Do you look them in the eye when you're listening?

3 Which parts of someone else's body is it acceptable to touch in everyday circumstances?

4 When do you shake someone's hand?

5 When do you smile at someone?

6 When you're with someone you don't know, how long can you remain silent before you feel obliged to start talking again?

7 What clothes do you wear to school or work? Are they different from clothes you wear at home?

8 How many ways can you say 'no' without speaking?

9 How many ways can you say 'well done' without speaking?

10 What do you do to make someone feel welcome in your home?

Work in groups of three or four. Discuss your answers. Did you all have the same answers?

3 How can you create a positive impression on someone? Decide which of the following ways you consider to be most effective. Put them in order from 1 (not very effective) to 10 (very effective).

- body posture
- clothing
- facial gestures
- hand gestures
- intonation
- jewellery and accessories
- physical appearance
- language
- loudness of the voice
- physical contact

Discuss your answers in your group. Try to reach agreement or agree to differ. Complete your exchange of views within four minutes.

In Phase C of the Speaking Paper, candidates are often given a problem-solving task to do together; this may be a series of points to place in order of importance. Here is what the interlocutor is likely to say.

Here is a list of situations and different means of communication. Discuss with your partner which you think are the most suitable means of communication for the different situations and why. You must reach agreement or agree to differ. After four minutes you must report your conclusion.

This phase focuses on your negotiation skills. It is important to know that the assessor and the interlocutor will be looking to see how well you collaborate and negotiate with your partner. But it isn't necessary to agree at all costs! Remember that the exam is testing your ability to manipulate English coherently and effectively, not your general knowledge or your social compatibility! Do make sure, however, that you give your partner time to talk and take your chance to do so as well.

In Phase D of the exam, both the interlocutor and the assessor may join in your discussion, and you may be asked more questions relating to the task. So, if you didn't speak much in Phase C, the examiners may direct more questions at you. It also allows the examiners to check their impressions of your level.

4 *Exam Question* The examiner will ask you and your partner to have a discussion about 'The most effective means of communication'. You must reach agreement or agree to differ. At the end of four minutes you will be asked to report your decision to the examiners.

Imagine that you need to decide which are the most effective means of communication in a variety of situations:

- inviting a friend for a meal
- a bomb warning at a railway station
- inviting your boss for an evening meal
- a complaint to the head office of a tourist agency
- informing a friend of last minute changes in travel arrangements
- a clothes retailer putting in an order for stock
- a foreign news correspondent sending an article to a newspaper

With your partner, discuss the means of communication listed below and try to agree on their suitability for the situations above.

- a letter
- a telephone call
- a fax message
- a face-to-face meeting
- a gift such as flowers or chocolate
- a TV advert
- a newspaper announcement

5 Summarise your arguments from activity 4 and present them to the rest of the class. Can anyone think of anything which you have left out?

UNIT

5

Unusual occupations

Section A Listening

The aim of this section is to focus on the following.
- listening for stress on important words for meaning
- predicting and listening for details of a passage

The exam question prepares you for Section C of the exam; it requires you to complete sentences with information from a recording by writing a word or a short phrase.

1 ⚏ Work in pairs. Look at the photos of people who have unusual jobs. What do you think they do?

Which of the words in the list below would you use to talk about these jobs?

aroma balcony bank branches canal Chanel conservation
cosmetics cottage create fishing flooding fragrance garden
gondola heart heights horticulture love navigation *nez*
opera Paris passion park perfume repertoire river rope
roses safety harness scent style tenor tropical voice

Underline any words which are not suitable for describing any of the jobs.

STUDY TIP

In English, speakers usually stress the information they consider to be important. If you can recognise when a person does this, it will help you identify this important information. Remember that you do not need to understand every word in order to grasp the important points. For example:

— When you ask someone a question, they are likely to stress the words which answer the question in their answer.

— In most instances, words which convey lexical meaning are more likely to be stressed than words which convey grammatical meaning.

2 Read the first part of an interview with a lock-keeper. With your partner, think about the questions and decide which words are likely to be stressed in the answers.

- **How long have you been a lock-keeper, Mr Fielder?**
- Oh dear, let me think – umm – I started when I was 25, so that means I've been at it for uh twenty-one years now. Yeah, that's it – three years on the Oxford canal and the past eighteen years here on the Reading stretch. Twenty-one years in all.
- **What did you do before you became a lock-keeper?**
- I used to be an electrician. That's what I trained as.
- **Do you ever regret leaving your profession?**
- Oh, no. Absolutely not. Right from the start I realised this was the one job that I would love to do. And I was right.
- **When is your most busy time of year?**
- The summer months. I can easily work a ten-hour day with all the holiday traffic and the upkeep of the flower beds along the side of the lock.

🔲 🔑 Listen to the recording and check your answers.

3 Read the second part of the interview. With your partner, try and guess the missing words.

- **Many people imagine life on the river as uneventful and easy-going. Is this right?**
- Yes, ... often ...... me if I ever get ...... sitting around here! In fact, I .... at six most mornings, and even in ...... when there are fewer ...... about, there is a lot to do controlling the water .... When it ...... hard in the ...... , I can be up half a dozen times attending to the weir .... No, I'm afraid the popular image of the pipe-smoking old man, ... against the lock gate ...... for the occasional ...... is far from the truth.

⌨ ☎ Listen to the recording and check your answers.

Did you find it difficult to guess the missing words? If so, can you explain why?

4 You are going to hear an interview with a professional serenader. Read the first part of the interview and underline the words that are important for meaning.

- I believe you are the founder of Serenading Service – is that right?
- Yes, that's right. I started the service three years ago when I realised that British people were desperate for romance with a capital 'R'. I thought there would be a clientele for a hired serenader.
- **How did you begin your career as a singer?**
- I started singing as a choirboy and at the age of ten I was chosen to sing alongside Placido Domingo at a charity do. That's what really got me started on a musical career. I went on to study music and then I joined an Opera company.

⌨ ☎ Listen to the recording and find out if the words you underlined were stressed by the speakers.

5 Read the second part of the interview. With your partner, try and guess the missing words. Can you understand the meaning without the complete text?

- **Where did the idea of serenading come from?**
- From ...... studies ...... Renaissance music, ... , ... course, opera, which is full ...... serenades. On the continent, especially ...... Spain ...... Italy where it still thrives, it .... traditional romantic experience. Over ...... centuries, university students ...... turned the serenade .... art form ...... hire.
- **What exactly do you do?**
- Well, usually I am hired ...... men ...... sing love songs ...... women. Occasionally I ...... asked ...... sing ...... men, but only ...... exceptionally.

⌨ ☎ Listen to the recording and check your answers.

Did you find it easier to guess the missing words in this extract than in the extract in activity 3? If so, can you explain why?

6 📼 🎧 Listen to the final part of the interview. Find the answers to these questions.

1 What sort of songs does the serenader sing?
2 Where does he sing from?
3 How much do the services of a serenader cost?
4 How do people usually react?
5 How do serenaders avoid unpleasant situations?

Compare your answers with your partner. Then listen to the recording again and check.

7 📼 🎧 *Exam Question* You will hear a radio interview with a man who is a professional tree-climber. Look at the sentences and complete them by writing one or two words in the spaces. Listen carefully. You will hear this piece twice.

Mr Saw has been a tree surgeon and qualified tree-climber for | 1 | .

He started climbing trees for the Parks department when he was | 2 | .

He was well adapted to climbing trees because he was | 3 | and he was not afraid | 4 | .

He went to Merristwood College in Surrey, where he followed a course on tree | 5 | climbing.

His work is varied. He may be asked to | 6 | or to conduct | 7 | on the tree.

Last year he worked for a | 8 | .

He travelled to the Comoros Islands and climbed a | 9 | in order to catch a | 10 | .

He has never | 11 | .

He has climbed trees more than | 12 | high.

He is now a lecturer on | 13 | at a horticultural college.

8 Would you like to do any of the jobs mentioned in this unit? Do you have the qualities necessary for any of the jobs?

Section B Speaking

The aim of this section is to focus on the following.

– describing and commenting on a photo

The exam question prepares you for Phase B of the exam; it requires you to describe and identify two photos in a series.

1 Look at the words you underlined in Section A, activity 1. What job(s) do you think these words could describe?

Write down five or six questions you could ask someone with this job.

2 Read the description below of a job. It is a job which the underlined words could be used to describe.

Caroline is a perfume creator or *nez* and she lives and works in Paris for a German company. She develops new aromas for cosmetics and perfumes. All the raw materials are imported from the South of France so it makes sense to live in Paris for someone in this line of work. Paris is a city that offers ideas and Caroline finds most of her inspiration by looking at people. Parisian women display more style than others and just seem to know how to put everything together and make it look great. They are not afraid of taking risks.

An important aspect of Caroline's work is to evaluate how much women's perception of beauty is influenced by advertising and magazines and how this is reflected in what they buy.

Her own personal favourite perfume is Chanel No. 5, a great classic. Her husband is also a perfume creator and they live and work side by side. He creates beautiful and very successful fragrances, but Caroline doesn't usually wear any of them.

Did you think of this type of work? Does the article answer your questions?

3 Write down the questions the interviewer asked Caroline before writing the description of her job.

Examples: *What do you do? Where do you work?*

4 Work in pairs. Act out the interview with Caroline using the questions you wrote in activity 3.

Change roles and act out the interview again.

5 With your partner, choose four of the jobs from the list below. Think of four or five words you can use to talk about each job. Write the words in four separate groups on a piece of paper.

> bank clerk   carpenter   computer programmer   dancer   decorator
> film director   gardener   head teacher   newspaper editor
> orchestra conductor   shop assistant   telephone salesperson
> wine maker

Work with another pair of students. Exchange your pieces of paper. Can you guess which jobs your partners were thinking of?

6 Look at the photo below. With your partner, describe the photo in as much detail as possible. Take turns to make sentences giving one piece of information about it. Score one point for each piece of information. Who scores more points?

EXAM TIP

Phase B of the interview usually involves candidates in describing a picture. The variation in the Exam question in activity 7 involves both candidates having the same set of pictures although they may be in a different order. Candidate A is asked to choose two pictures and describe them. Candidate B is then asked to identify which pictures Candidate A has chosen. This is what the interlocutor is likely to say.

*In this part of the test, I'm going to give each of you some pictures to look at. Please do not show your pictures to each other. You each have pictures of the same scenes but your pictures are in a different order. Candidate A, I'd like you to choose **two** pictures and describe them as fully as possible so that Candidate B can identify them. You have about a minute to do this.*

*Candidate B, I'd like you to listen carefully and decide which **two** pictures are being described. If you are still uncertain after Candidate A has finished, you may ask him/her questions to help you identify the pictures. Otherwise I'd like you to say briefly what helped you recognise the pictures.*

After approximately a minute of Candidate A's description, the interlocutor may say:
Candidate B, have you decided which pictures Candidate A was describing? Would you like to check and compare your pictures?

Remember that this phase of the interview involves one or the other candidate speaking at some length and without the usual turn-taking which occurs in most everyday speech. Practise giving these longer descriptions in class as much as you can, so that you feel at ease with them before you go into the interview.

After such an exam question, there may be a similar activity or one like that in Unit 2 to allow Candidate B the opportunity to speak at length.

7 *Exam Question*   Work in pairs. You are going to look at some photos. Please do not show your photos to each other.
Student A: Turn to page 87.
Student B: Turn to page 88.

8 Repeat activity 7 to allow Student B the opportunity to speak.

STUDENT A: Turn to page 89.
STUDENT B: Turn to page 90.

UNIT 6

Food and eating habits

Section A Listening

The aim of this section is to focus on the following.

- inferring what people mean from tone of voice and the choice of language
- listening for specific information

The exam question prepares you for Section B of the exam; it gives you one opportunity only to complete a chart with specific information from a recording.

1 Look at the photos below. Work in small groups. Discuss what sort of food you would expect to eat in these restaurants. Decide which you would choose for the following.

- a working lunch
- a celebration dinner
- a family meal
- a quick snack
- an evening out with friends

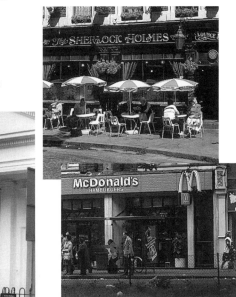

STUDY TIP

People don't always say what they mean, they sometimes say things indirectly. For example, when someone is criticising something or somebody, they may try not to sound too negative in order to avoid hurting people's feelings. Rather than saying exactly what they think, they may begin by mentioning possible explanations or special circumstances. For example, instead of saying that something was dreadful, they may use expressions like *disappointing* or *not up to expectations*. In this case the listener has to infer the full meaning from what the speaker actually says.

Tone of voice is also a useful indication of how people feel about things. For example, if someone is talking enthusiastically about a meal they had, they may not actually state that the restaurant was excellent, but you can infer this from the way they speak about their evening out.

2 **You are going to hear a conversation in which two people are talking about restaurants.**

Listen to the recording. Put *S* if the speakers were satisfied, *D* if they were dissatisfied, and *N* if they haven't been to the restaurant in the chart below.

	Restaurant	*Opinion*	*Comments*
Man	Gilbey's		
	Golden Bengal		
	Gino's		
Woman	Gilbey's		
	Golden Bengal		
	Gino's		

Listen to the recording again. Note down the speakers' positive and negative comments in the chart above.

Which restaurant would you like to try? Which would you avoid? Be prepared to explain your reasons to the class.

3 **Work in groups of three or four. Talk about the last time you went to a restaurant. Consider the following questions.**

– When and why did you go?
– Who did you go with?
– What was the interior and the atmosphere like?
– What was the food and the service like?
– What did you particularly like or dislike about the restaurant?

EXAM TIP

You will be required to answer the type of exam question below in Section B of the exam. These questions test your ability to understand specific information. The questions are always in the order of the text. The main difficulty is that you will only hear the recording once. It is therefore essential to study the chart very carefully to make sure you know exactly what sort of information you are listening for. But remember that within the text there will be some repetition, so there may be a second chance to extract the necessary information.

4 Work in pairs. Look carefully at the chart in activity 5. For each blank in the chart, decide which of the following you are listening for.

  a yes or no answer   a number   one or a few words

5 🖭 🎧 *Exam Question*   You will hear part of a telephone conversation in which a person from a tourist office is giving details of two restaurants to the organiser of a seminar. As you listen, fill in the information for items 1–10. You will need to write yes or no, a number, or a few words. Some of the information has been completed for you. Listen carefully as you will hear this piece once only.

	The Walnut Tree	Europa Hotel
Location	5 km from centre	1
Separate room for large groups	No	2
Cost per person	3	4
Wine included	5	No
Type of cooking	6	7
Vegetarian menu	8	9
Present rating	10	two star

6 Work in small groups. Imagine you are organising a seminar for about 30 people. What points would you consider important for the choice of restaurant for the participants' last evening?

Would you consider either of the restaurants described above?

Section B Speaking

The aim of this section is to focus on the following.

- using paraphrase to replace words you don't know
- comparing and problem solving

The exam question prepares you for Phase B of the exam; it requires you to describe and compare two similar photos.

1 Answer the questions in the questionnaire below.

How important is food to you?

1 How do you eat?

A I have three meals at fixed times every day.
B I never sit down to a meal but I nibble all day.
C I have one main meal in the evening.
D I have no regular routine for mealtimes.

2 What do you usually eat at lunch time?

A nothing
B a quick snack in a café
C a complete meal at a restaurant or canteen
D home-made sandwiches

3 Would you say that you are:

A a good cook?
B an adventurous cook?
C no good at all?
D only able to cook very basic food?

4 If you invited a friend to dinner, would you:

A cook the meal yourself?
B get someone else to do the cooking?
C buy a take-away meal from a local restaurant?
D buy a frozen meal and heat it up in the micro-wave?

5 When you go out for a meal, do you choose:

A straightforward home-type food?
B exotic or unusual food?
C a McDonald's or some other fast food chain?
D somewhere cheap?

6 How do you choose a restaurant?

A You only try a restaurant that has been recommended by someone you know.
B You consult a good food guide.
C You only go to restaurants within walking distance of your home.
D You go on appearances and try restaurants that look attractive.

7 Which statement best expresses your attitude to food and diet?

A I only eat because I have to.
B Food is a great pleasure.
C I am very careful about what I eat; I make sure that my diet is healthy.
D I'm not particularly concerned about what I eat, as long as it is tasty.

Work in groups. Compare your answers. Check your scores on page 127.

STUDY TIP

When you can't remember or don't know a word, you probably get around the difficulty by explaining what you mean in a few words – you use paraphrase. You also use paraphrase when someone asks you to explain to them the meaning of a word or expression.

For an object, you may want to describe its appearance, its function or what it is made of. Here are some phrases which you may find useful:

It's a thing you use for … .
You use it for … .
It's for … .
It's a thing for … .
It looks like … .
It's (a bit) like … .
It's made of … .

When the word is not an object, you can illustrate meaning by giving examples of the use of the word or expression in context. For example:

It's a feeling you have when … .
You feel X when … .

2 Work in pairs. If you are in Britain, work with a student from a different country. Design a detailed menu for one day which would satisfy you both. Make sure you reach agreement on meal times, amounts of food, drinks etc.

When you have finished, present your menu to the rest of the class.

Were there any points where you found it difficult to reach agreement? Was this because of personal taste or national habits?

3 With another pair of students, compare the menus you designed in activity 2. How could you improve them from a health point of view?

Discuss the following points.

animal proteins   quantity   fat   fibre   fruit and vegetables
number of meals a day   carbohydrates (sugar and starch)   vitamins

How would you modify your menus for the following people?

diabetics   Hindus   Muslims   small children
someone who is overweight

4 Look at these two menus. In your group, discuss what is wrong with them.

8 am: *a fried breakfast with eggs,*
        bacon, sausage, tomatoes
        3 slices of toast and butter
        2 cups of sweet tea
 	
11 am: *cup of coffee, bar of milk*
        chocolate
 	
1 pm: *4 ham sandwiches, packet*
        of crisps, piece of cake, beer
 	
4 pm: *piece of cake, tea*
 	
7 pm: *evening meal: chips,*
        carrots, steak
        rice pudding, tea
	8 am:
	     black coffee,
	     an apple
	
	12 midday:
	     tomato salad, ham, a pear,
	     black coffee
	
	8 pm:
	     bowl of vegetable soup,
	     cheese, wine

Decide which menu is healthier. How could the menus be improved?

How healthy is your own diet? How could you improve it?

EXAM TIP

In Unit 3, it was mentioned that Spot the difference was a common task type in Phase B. Turn back to page 24 to remind yourself of what the examiner might say. If you are nervous about the interview, it is important to remember that the examiners are not looking to fail you or mark you down. They have been trained to give you as fair a mark as they can using the assessment criteria. Whenever you have the chance, use the Assessment grid (on page 99) to evaluate the level and the progress of your colleagues, and to share that information with them. Remember also that it is the examiner's job to make sure you both get enough opportunities to speak during the interview. They may therefore intervene in order to adjust the balance in favour of any candidate who has not had the chance to show his or her speaking ability.

5 *Exam Question*   Work in groups of three.

STUDENT A: You are the examiner. Listen to Candidates B and C and use the Assessment grid on page 99 to help you form an impression of their level.
STUDENT B: Turn to page 91.
STUDENT C: Turn to page 92.

6 Repeat activity 6 to allow **Student A** the opportunity to speak.

STUDENT A: Turn to page 93.
STUDENT B: Turn to page 94.
STUDENT C: You are the examiner. Listen to Candidates A and B and use the Assessment grid on page 99 to help you form an impression of their level.

7 In your group, talk about the kind of food you like to eat, and the kind of food you should eat more or less of. Discuss the following questions.

- Do you enjoy cooking?
- How often do people prepare food for you?
- How often do you go out to a restaurant?

7

Expressing your opinions

Section A Listening

The aim of this section is to focus on the following.
- listening for specific information
- inferring meaning from tone of voice and attitude

The exam question prepares you for Section D of the exam; it requires you to match extracts with topics and to match extracts with speakers' reactions.

1 What is your attitude to taking part in surveys and opinion polls? Look at the questions below and answer them.

---

1   When was the last time you answered a survey?

- I can't remember   – never
- not long ago   – other
- ages ago

2   Which of these types of surveys and opinion polls have you taken part in in the past?

a) a questionnaire about your personal qualities in a magazine
b) a market research questionnaire about a new product in a supermarket
c) an on-the-spot citizen survey about services or facilities available in a public place, e.g. town centre, airport, station
d) a political opinion poll survey
e) a questionnaire over the phone
f) a national population census

3   What is your attitude to questionnaires and surveys?

a) I refuse to answer.
b) I answer but I do not tell the truth.
c) I answer as truthfully as I can.
d) I never give my name and address.
e) I think of an excuse.
f) I enjoy answering.

Work in pairs. Compare your answers. Explain the reasons for your answers to question 3.

2 You are going to hear somebody asking three members of the public questions about the facilities at an airport.

Look at the headings in the chart below with your partner. Write down the questions the interviewer is likely to ask.

	Speaker 1	*Speaker 2*	*Speaker 3*
Destination	Barcelona		
Reason for travel			
User frequency			
Refreshments			
Speed of formalities			
Parking facilities			
Transport to the airport			
Signposting			

⌷ ⌸ Listen to the recording and complete the chart.

Compare your answers with your partner. Then listen to the recording again and check your answers. Are the interviewer's questions similar to those you wrote down? Which speaker is most positive about the airport?

Which speaker is least positive? How can you explain such widely different opinions?

3 With your partner, ask and answer questions about an airport, a railway station or a bus station you know. Use the headings in the chart in activity 2 to help you.

EXAM TIP

In Section D, you will hear a number of short extracts and will be asked to answer two series of questions. The first series is generally a straightforward matching task as in Task 1 in activity 4, where you are asked to match extracts with topics. In the second series, the answers may not be stated clearly and you may have to infer meaning.

It is usually difficult to do the two tasks simultaneously. The recording is played twice so you may find it easier to concentrate on one task at a time. You may find the followings steps helpful:

– Read Task 1 and the different options carefully.
– Read Task 2 and the different options carefully.
– Listen and answer Task 1; re-read the options for Task 2.
– Listen and answer Task 2; check and correct Task 1 as you listen.

4 🔲 🔴 *Exam Question*   You will hear various people talking. They are being interviewed on a variety of topics. You will hear the people twice.

Task 1
Look at the topics listed below. As you listen, decide in what order you hear them mentioned and complete the boxes with the appropriate letter. Three topics will not be used.

A voting intentions
B TV viewing survey
C political popularity poll
D marriage agency questionnaire
E unemployment agency questionnaire
F survey for fast food products
G local facilities survey
H travel agency questionnaire

1	
2	
3	
4	
5	

Task 2
Look at the speakers' reactions listed below. As you listen put the reactions in the order in which you hear them mentioned. Three reactions will not be used.

A refuses rudely because s/he does not
   approve of this type of survey.
B accepts reluctantly.
C answers willingly but is doubtful of the
   relevance to him/her of the questionnaire.
D answers enthusiastically because the
   topic interests him/her.
E refuses rudely and tells the interviewer
   to go away.
F accepts at first, then refuses to continue
   when s/he realises what the subject is.
G refuses apologetically because s/he is in a hurry.
H accepts willingly but doesn't answer the questions.

6	
7	
8	
9	
10	

5 How would you react if you were asked to answer questions on the topics in Task 1 in activity 4? Explain your reasons to another student.

Section B Speaking

The aim of this section is to focus on the following.

- asking for explanations and clarifications of words or ideas
- ranking and reaching agreement, reporting decisions

The exam question prepares you for Phase C of the exam; it requires you to comment on a photo and discuss purpose. It also prepares you for Phase D; it requires you to report your decisions.

1 Answer these questions.

> **How do you express yourself?**
> - Do you enjoy controversial discussions?
> - Do you easily change your views in the course of a discussion?
> - Do you tend to impose your views on others?
> - Do you find it difficult to express your opinions in public?
> - Are there areas where you have very strong views?
> - Are there subjects which you avoid?
> - What are your favourite discussion topics?
> - Do you like to shock other people by expressing ideas you don't necessarily believe in?

Work in pairs. How well do you know your partner? Try to predict your partner's answers to the questions.

With your partner, ask and answer the questions. How accurate were your predictions?

2 Look at the topics below with your partner. Which of these topics do you consider to be suitable for an English study book for students from a wide variety of countries? Which topics do you consider to be unsuitable? Explain your reasons.

> cultural differences   death   divorce and marriage   drugs
> education   entertainment   freedom of speech   health   holidays
> international politics   literature   love and sex   religion   sport
> terrorism   wildlife

Write down a few more suitable and unsuitable topics.

3 Work with another pair of students. Report the discussion you had in activity 2 and explain your views. Find out if the other pair agree with your choice of topics.

4 In your groups, look at the different units in this book and put the topics in order of interest. Try to reach agreement.

Sometimes it is difficult to understand what someone says, so it is useful to have a series of set formulae ready to use. If you use them properly, they may even add to the impression of fluency, which is an important aspect of the interview. Here are some of the formulae you can use:

Sorry, I don't understand.

(I beg your) pardon?

What did you say, please?

(Sorry) could you say that again, please?

Could you repeat that, please?

(Sorry, +) Wh-question

(Sorry, +) Why did you say+interrogative clause?

Did you say X?

Do you mean to say + that clause?

(Sorry,) what does X mean?

What do you mean by X?

What is X?

Could you explain that, please?

5 ⌐o *Exam question*   Look at the photo below. With your partner, talk about the photo and decide what is going on. Try and guess the purpose of the people's behaviour, who it is aimed at and how effective you think it is. Do you agree with this sort of action?

You have three or four minutes to do this.

6 Work with another pair of students. Report the decisions you made in activity 5 to your partners. Find out whether they agree with your ideas.

Give your opinions with one person in the group directing the discussion. Think about the following points.

- Would you be prepared to take part in a similar protest action?
- If so, what ideas would you be prepared to defend in this way?
- If not, how would you express your opinions?

7 In your group, discuss the following ways of protesting.

go-slow actions   non-violent resistance   road blocks
street demonstrations   strikes   terrorist action   violence
work-to-rule

8 In your group, read the Exam Tip below and discuss the following questions.

- Which criteria do you feel most confident about?
- What do you need more work on?
- What types of activities are useful for developing the speaking criteria?

Look at the Assessment grid on page 99 and discuss your levels. What activity types would most benefit you?

EXAM TIP

There are five criteria for assessment. Look at the Assessment grid on page 99 as you read this.

Fluency This refers to the speed and rhythm of your speech, and the lack of hesitation. Short pauses which suggest you are organising your thoughts will not be penalised.

Accuracy This relates to the range and correctness of the grammar and vocabulary you use. Remember that mistakes which do not hinder communication will not be heavily penalised.

Pronunciation This covers individual sounds, stress and intonation in words and sentences. You won't be expected to conceal all influences of your native language.

Task achievement This focuses attention on how successfully you have carried out the task without prompting from the examiners and in an organised, flexible way. But above all, it is the process of achieving the task more than the achievement itself which will interest the examiners.

Interactive communication This refers to the candidate's ability to lead and participate in discussions. Taking turns to speak is important, and any candidate who attempts to dominate the interview will lose marks.

UNIT

8

Leadership

Section A Listening

The aim of this section is to focus on the following.

– understanding text organisation and following the thread of a passage by recognising discourse markers
– listening for detail
– listening for main ideas

The exam question prepares you for Section D of the exam; it requires you to match extracts with people and to match extracts with personal qualities.

1 ⌗0 Work in pairs. Can you name the leaders from the past in the photos? Which countries did they come from?

Add one or two names to the list. Then put all the leaders in order of how great you consider they were. What made these people great leaders?

1

2

3

4

5

6

7

8

9

10

STUDY TIP

When people have to speak for quite a long time – when making a speech, giving a report, or giving a detailed explanation, for example – they are likely to use a number of techniques to organise their ideas and make it easier for the listener to follow what they are saying. They may use words or phrases to indicate what the next stage of the speech or explanation will be. These are called discourse markers, and they help guide the listener through the speech or explanation. For example:

– when listing points: *first, first of all, to start with, secondly, finally, also, then*
– before an explanation: *in other words, I mean*
– to give an example: *(take) … , for example, for instance, like, such as*
– when presenting another side to an issue: *on the other hand, but, however*
– when presenting results: *as a result, so*
– to summarise ideas: *so you see, in conclusion, to sum up*

Speakers may also ask a question and then go on to answer it. At the end of a long answer or explanation, they may summarise what they have been saying. You may find it useful to practise listening out for these discourse markers which are also likely to be of use to you when you have to do the speaking!

2 **You are going to hear an extract from a radio interview with a historian who is talking about the characteristics of leaders. Which of the words below do you think the speaker is likely to use?**

> history great ambition fun side politician holiday hero teacher tyrant unhappy soldier work outstanding warrior countryside business follower plunder wartime spiritual dangerous madman unemployment

🔲 ⏻ **Listen to the recording. Underline the words the speaker uses.**

3 ⏻ **Read the tapescript below. What words or phrases does the speaker use to organise what he is saying?**

Well, to start with, I think we can learn a lot from history by studying the great men and women who've left their mark at different times – for both good and bad, I hasten to add. But, of course, many of the great leaders of the past were military chiefs, and depending on whose side you found yourself on, they were either national heroes or, er, dreaded tyrants. Take Genghis Khan, for example, he was undoubtedly an outstanding warrior and military leader, if you happened to be one of his followers, that is. But if you were unlucky enough to live in a country he plundered, you were more likely to see him as a dangerous madman. So you see, not everyone is likely to see these so-called great leaders in the same light.

4 ☐ ⏻ Listen to the second part of the interview. Complete the gaps in the transcript.

- But were all the great leaders of the past military chiefs?
- Oh no, of course there were ...... the great spiritual leaders who have changed the world. Men ...... Luther and Gandhi. ...... I think it is true to say that most people, even today, continue to identify great leadership with military models. ...... , just consider the criticisms our politicians get fired at them. How often do we hear them being compared unfavourably to wartime heroes such as Churchill or de Gaulle? Even though the job at hand is very different. What good would military strategy be for dealing with unemployment? I'm pretty sure it would be of little use. ...... even though these models no longer bear any relation to the complex workings of the modern world, we still measure ministers or company directors against them.

What other techniques does the speaker use to signal to the listener what he is going to say next?

5 ☐ ⏻ Listen to the final part of the interview. Put the characteristics which the speaker suggests are common to all successful leaders in the order in which he mentions them.

a) Successful leaders achieve their goals.
b) They are prepared to do anything to achieve their objectives.
c) They know exactly what their objectives are.
d) Their objectives are always for the good of ordinary people.
e) They maintain absolute concentration on their aim.

Listen to the recording again. Note down the words or phrases that the speaker uses to list the different characteristics.

6 With your partner, discuss the qualities listed below. Choose five or six which you think are essential for a successful leader – be it a football team captain or a company executive. Try to agree on their order of importance.

ambition   arrogance   authority   compassion   courage
determination   enthusiasm   generosity   honesty   impartiality
intelligence   self-confidence   self-discipline   sense of humour
single-mindedness

7 Work in groups of three or four. Describe people that you know and particularly admire for their qualities as leaders. Can you agree on the Top Ten Most Impressive Leaders?

8 *Exam Question* You will hear various speakers talking about people they admire for their leadership qualities. You will hear the speakers twice.

Task 1
Look at the types of leader listed below. As you listen, decide in what order you hear them mentioned and complete the boxes with the appropriate letter. Three speakers will not be used.

A Research team leader
B Football manager
C Military officer
D TV Director of programmes
E Museum director
F Head of an advertising agency
G Politician
H School headmaster

1	
2	
3	
4	
5	

Task 2
Look at the leadership qualities listed below. As you listen, put the qualities in the order in which you hear them mentioned and complete the boxes with the appropriate letter. Three qualities will not be used.

A a good listener
B intellectual courage
C very decisive
D a clear knowledge of goals
E ability to delegate
G very determined
F a sense of humour
H dislikes unpleasant behaviour

6	
7	
8	
9	
10	

9 Do the speakers in activity 8 mention any of the qualities you chose in activity 2?

Section B Speaking

The aim of this section is to focus on the following.

– answering a questionnaire, comparing and explaining answers
– expressing opinions and compromising and coming to acceptable conclusions

The exam question prepares you for Phase C of the exam; it requires you to discuss and express agreement or disagreement with statements. It also prepares you for Phase D; it requires you to report the conclusions of a discussion.

1 The questionnaire below is designed to help you assess your potential for leadership and decide whether this is the role for you. Answer the questions.

Are you a leader?

1 **When new people join in a group or organisation with which you are involved, do you:**
   a) wait for someone else to introduce them?
   b) make them feel welcome?
   c) find out more about them to help them fit in?

2 **If you are working with people less experienced than yourself, do you:**
   a) offer lots of advice and encouragement?
   b) tell them exactly what to do and how to do it?
   c) let them get on with it?

3 **In the family in which you grew up, were you:**
   a) the oldest or the only child?
   b) the youngest child?
   c) somewhere in the middle?

4 **Have you ever experienced any of the following? (Tick as many as apply):**
   a) been elected as a shop steward or staff representative?
   b) been captain of a sports team?
   c) been asked to represent your group at another meeting?

5 **Imagine the car of your dreams. Would you most like to be:**
   a) the driver?
   b) the passenger?
   c) the designer?

6 **If you were working in a group on a difficult task, would you:**
   a) hope someone else would tell you what to do?
   b) describe in glowing terms the purpose of the task?
   c) seek to establish deadlines and schedules?

7 **When confronted by a really difficult decision, do you:**
   a) find something else to do?
   b) ask other people for their advice?
   c) make your mind up quickly?

8 **Confronted by puzzling problems, do you provide others with:**
   a) very little help?
   b) new ways of looking at them?
   c) a systematic approach to problem solving?

Work in pairs. Try and guess how your partner answered the questions. Compare your answers and the reasons for your choice.

STUDY TIP

When you discuss a problem with other people in order to take a decision, you usually try to come to a conclusion which is acceptable to everyone. During the discussion you probably express your personal views and try and convince people of your opinions: you also say whether or not you agree with other people's ideas.

If you don't all agree on every point, you will probably all have to make compromises. This is a process of 'give and take', which involves deciding what you can and cannot accept and coming to final agreement. In this sort of discussion it is important to listen to other people and not try to impose your views on them by talking too much or too loudly!

2 **Which answers in the questionnaire in activity 1 do you think suggest leadership potential? With your partner, complete the scoring grid below with the figures 0, 1 or 2 according to how little or how much leadership potential the answers reveal.**

Scores

1: (a)...... (b)...... (c)......   5: (a)...... (b)...... (c)......

2: (a)...... (b)...... (c)......   6: (a)...... (b)...... (c)......

3: (a)...... (b)...... (c)......   7: (a)...... (b)...... (c)......

4: (a)...... (b)...... (c)......   8: (a)...... (b)...... (c)......

Work with another pair of students. Explain your choices. Discuss any differences and come to a final group decision on the scoring system.

Turn to page 128 and work out your own score. Do any of you have leadership potential? Do any of you already have a leader's role in your professional or personal life?

3 Look at the general statements below about leadership.

– Leaders are born and not made.
– Leadership is an out-dated male myth.
– Leaders are chosen by their followers.
– It is better to have an army of rabbits commanded by a lion than an army of lions commanded by a rabbit.
– Good followers make good leaders.

Discuss the statements with your partner. Find out which you agree with and which you disagree with. Make sure that you understand your partner's views by asking him or her to explain anything you are not clear about as you go along.

EXAM TIP

In Phase D of the exam you are asked to report your own and your partner's opinions and say whether you agree or have different opinions. Start with an overall comment summarising the general outcome of the discussion, for example, *We both agreed with a number of statements but not with ... .* The discussion may develop into general considerations about the subject. Remember that the assessor, who will have been relatively silent until this point, may join in the discussion. This will allow him or her to get a more accurate impression of your speaking ability.

4 *Exam Question* Work in groups of four. Do not work with the partner you worked with in activity 3.

STUDENTS A and B: You are exam candidates. Discuss the statements about leadership in activity 3. Find out which you agree with and which you disagree with.
STUDENTS C and D: You are examiners. Listen to Candidates A and B and use the Assessment grid on page 99 to help you form an impression of their level.

5 Repeat activity 4 to allow Students C and D the opportunity to speak. Change roles.

UNIT 9

Environmental hazards

Section A Listening

The aim of this section is to focus on the following.

- inferring and interpreting the attitude of speakers from language features such as the tone of voice, speed of speech, hesitation
- listening for specific information

The exam question prepares you for Section D of the exam; it requires you to match extracts with speakers and to match extracts with topics.

1 Work in pairs. Look at the photo below of a sinking oil-tanker. Have you read about a similar disaster? Do you know why the ship sank? What were the consequences?

2 You are going to hear a report about tanker disasters. Work in pairs. List possible causes of tanker disasters. Do you think that most accidents could be avoided or are some inevitable?

▭ ⌕ Listen to the recording. What are the main causes of disasters mentioned in the report? Did you include them in your list?

3 🎧 Listen to the recording again and complete the chart below.

Name	Date of Sinking	Age of Tanker	Location
Aegean Sea			
Exxon Valdez			
Katina P			
Kirki			

STUDY TIP

When you speak, you communicate information both verbally (with words) and non-verbally (by your attitude, reactions, expressions and gestures). A great deal of information is conveyed by the way you speak: tone of voice, speed of speech, silences, hesitations, pauses, repetitions etc. In your own language all these different features of speech help you identify and interpret context.

Tone of voice can tell you about a speaker's attitude; long silences may indicate embarrassment or lack of confidence; many hesitations, pauses and repetitions may betray ignorance or misunderstanding; a speaker who interrupts and dominates a discussion may be over-confident or even arrogant.

When you listen to recorded material, if you are able to interpret the attitude of a speaker this can help you decide what type of person is speaking and what his or her role is. It will give you a better idea of the context of what you are listening to.

4 **Work in small groups. You are going to hear various people talking about a tanker disaster in activity 5. Before you listen to the recording, look at the list of people in activity 5 and discuss what their attitudes might be. You can use the following words or expressions.**

angry   business-like   confident   constructive   cynical
despairing   embarrassed   emotional   exaggerating   neutral
outraged   reassuring   resigned   unconcerned   unperturbed

What sort of comments are these people likely to make?

EXAM TIP

In Task 1 of the Exam question below, you have to recognise the type of person speaking. You don't need to understand details of what he or she is talking about but you do need to recognise the speaker's attitude. It is therefore useful to look carefully at the list of people and try to predict what their attitudes are likely to be and the sort of things they might say.

In Task 2, you don't need to remember specific details but you must identify the topics they are talking about. Before you listen, look carefully at the topics and think about the sort of things the five speakers in Task 1 are likely to be concerned with. In both tasks, there are extra options.

5 📼 🎤 *Exam Question*   You will hear various people talking about a tanker disaster. You will hear the people twice.

Task 1
Look at the types of person listed below. As you listen, decide in what order you hear them speak and complete the boxes with the appropriate letter. Three people will not be used.

A a Green party campaigner
B a member of the public
C a central government spokesman
D a local inhabitant of a disaster area
E a shipowner spokesman
F a radio newsreader
G a local official
H an insurance broker

1	
2	
3	
4	
5	

Task 2
Look at the topics listed below. As you listen, put the topics in the order in which you hear them mentioned and complete the boxes with the appropriate letter. Three topics will not be used.

A providing aid for the local people
B offering compensation payments
C preventing future disasters
D describing effect on local people's lives
E tightening international regulations
F criticising government policies
G keeping transport costs down
H explaining the cause of the accident

6	
7	
8	
9	
10	

6 In your group, imagine you are people from the list in activity 5. Act out interviews. Before you begin, decide what attitude you wish to convey by the tone of your voice and the way you speak.

7 In your group, imagine you are fishermen or local hotel owners. Plan and write a letter demanding compensation for the loss of trade caused by the oil spill.

Section B Speaking

The aim of this section is to focus on the following.

- expressing your views, listening and responding to counter arguments
- agreeing and disagreeing with other people's views

The exam question prepares you for Phase C of the exam; it requires you to rate things according to specified criteria.

1 Our modern lifestyles have made us dependent on large quantities of energy. What are the main sources of energy in your country? What alternatives are there?

2 Look at the opinions below. Which do you agree with? Which do you disagree with?

- Diversity is the key to independent and reliable energy supplies.
- Nuclear power plants for the production of electricity are the best modern option.
- Coal is out of date and dirty.
- Oil is a bad option because it leads to political and economic dependency.
- The future lies with solar energy.
- We should all start by reducing our energy consumption.

Work in pairs. Compare your opinions.

STUDY TIP

When participating in a discussion with people who hold different views from yourself, you probably include all or most of the following steps:

- expressing your views as clearly as possible
- listening attentively to what your interlocutor has to say
- responding appropriately with counter arguments
- recognising and agreeing with or refuting and disagreeing with their arguments

Informal discussions usually proceed in a succession of short exchanges rather than long speeches. This enables participants to follow the thread of the conversation and react and respond as they go along. So, remember not to speak for too long at a time and listen to what the other people have to say!

3 Choose a statement from activity 2 for which you and your partner have different views. Explain the reasons for your opinions and try to convince your partner that you are right. Make sure that you both speak for about the same amount of time and that you listen carefully to each other's arguments.

EXAM TIP

The next exam question is designed to test negotiation and collaboration skills, not your knowledge of industrial pollution! It can be seen as a sort of verbal game with a number of rules that should be followed.

Make sure that neither you nor your partner dominate the conversation. If necessary, encourage him or her to participate by asking questions.

If you do not understand a word or an idea, ask your partner to explain what he or she means.

4 *Exam question*   Work in groups of four.

STUDENTS A and B: Look at the list of installations below. Discuss the environmental consequences of each installation. Which have the most impact on the environment? Then decide which are likely to be the most unpleasant to live near and put them in order from 1 (most unpleasant) to 7 (least unpleasant). You must either reach agreement or agree to disagree. Make sure that you understand your partner's opinion.

- oil refinery
- nuclear power station
- nuclear recycling plant
- chemical plant
- industrial pig farm
- coal mine
- steel works

STUDENTS C and D: You are examiners. Listen to Candidates A and B. Think about what marks you would give them.

5 Discuss the candidates' performance. Focus on both positive and negative aspects. Make suggestions for improvement.

When you are ready, change roles. Repeat activity 4 to allow Students C and D the opportunity to speak.

6 In your group, look at the newspaper headlines below. What do you think they refer to? Write the outline of one of the articles.

Russians admit Deadliest leak since Chernobyl

Lethal legacy lies below icy waters

UNIT

10 Conscription

Section A Listening

The aim of this section is to focus on the following.

– listening for specific information

The exam question prepares you for Section A of the exam; it gives you one opportunity only to complete a chart with specific information from the recording.

1 This unit is about national service in different countries. Work in small groups. Discuss the following questions.

– Do you have conscription – compulsory military service – in your country? If so, how long does it last?
– Is there an alternative civilian service? If so, what sort of things do people do, and how long does it last?
– Have you done national service?

EXAM TIP

Section A of the exam usually consists of a monologue which lasts about two minutes. You will hear the recording twice. You may be asked to complete a chart with a number or a few words, as in the exam question in activity 3. The questions follow the order of the information and they are designed to test your ability to understand specific information. Because the questions are usually quite straightforward, you can answer as many as possible during the first listening and then check and complete your answers during the second listening. As always, make sure you read the questions carefully beforehand so that you know exactly what you are listening for.

2 Work in pairs. Read the Exam question in activity 3 and study the chart. For each blank in the chart, decide which of the following you are listening for.

age   a length of time   the name of a country

3 📼 ⌗0 *Exam Question*   You will hear a report on national service in different European countries. As you listen, fill in the information for items 1–10. Listen carefully. You will hear this piece twice.

	country	length of service
the longest	1	2
the shortest	3	4
no military service	5	
no alternative civilian service	6	
Length of annual national service in Switzerland	7	
End of annual service when men reach the age of	8	
Length of initial training in Switzerland	9	
which is normally done at the age of	10	

4 ⌗0   **With your partner, decide which of the following statements express ideas in favour of conscription.**

1 'It doesn't matter if the tanks don't work, as long as the men have neat uniforms and shiny boots.'
2 'Conscription ensures there is a close interaction between the army and society.'
3 'When you interrupt your studies to do something non-intellectual for a long time, it makes it difficult to start again.'
4 'A totally professional army is much more expensive to run than a conscripted army.'
5 'There are lots of military jobs which require very little training, such as driving jeeps, or carrying guns and conscripts can do them very well.'
6 'For many people it's the only opportunity they will ever have to mix with all sorts of different people.'
7 'It gives you a real sense of national identity.'
8 'There must be better ways of paying one's debt to society.'

5 You are going to hear three people expressing their views about conscription.

⊟ ⌐● Listen to the recording. Match the statements in activity 4 and the speakers.

Which speaker does not make any of the statements? What was this speaker's general opinion?

6 ⌐● Which of the words below would you use to describe the speakers in activity 5?

angry   concerned   enthusiastic   indifferent   left-wing
old-fashioned   passionate   right-wing

Compare your answers with your partner. Then listen to the recording from activity 5 again.

7 ⌐● With your partner, look at some more statements about military service.

1 'There is still a need for a conscripted military.'
2 'National service, yes, but not in the military.'
3 'It teaches young people self-respect and discipline.'
4 'It is a complete waste of time.'
5 'There are more worthwhile ways of contributing to society.'
6 'It disrupts studies or professional life.'
7 'It is useful for the country.'

Do you think the speakers in activity 5 would agree or disagree with the statements?

8 Discuss the questions below with your partner.

– Would you be prepared to fight for your country?
– Can you think of any circumstances in which you would refuse to take up arms?
– Do you think that a professional army is more likely than a conscripted army to fight for an unjustifiable cause?

Section B Speaking

The aim of this section is to focus on the following.

– discussing arguments for or against a controversial issue
– comparing opinions

The exam question prepares you for Phase C of the exam; it requires you to discuss statements and reach agreement or agree to disagree.

1 Work in pairs. Make a list of all the arguments for and against military service that have been mentioned by the different speakers in Section A.

Find out what your partner thinks about the statements in Section A, activity 4.

2 ⚏ Read the following newspaper article. Tick (✔) the issues in the list below which the article mentions. Then discuss these issues with your partner.

1 the punishment of people who refuse to do national service
2 conscientious objectors
3 national service for women
4 alternative civilian national service
5 overseas development service
6 the validity of military solutions in the modern world

SERVING TIME OVER A MATTER OF CONSCIENCE

The plight of the hundreds of conscientious objectors imprisoned across Europe highlights just how seriously governments take national service duties. Amnesty International say that as recently as 1990 half the nations of Europe imprisoned people for avoiding military service.

One country with very strict conscription laws is Greece, which has a longer military service than any other European country. As in Spain there is no alternative civilian form of national service, and on average more than 400 conscientious objectors are imprisoned every year.

The strong-arm methods used in Greece contrast sharply with Germany's law, which states: "No one may be compelled against his conscience to render war service involving the use of arms."

In 1989 Italy cut the length of time of alternative civilian service from 20 months to 12 months. Subsequently the number of people opting for civilian instead of military service rose dramatically from 8,000 to 30,000 a year.

In France where draft dodgers still receive tough prison sentences, there are plans to do away with compulsory military service altogether. Whether it will be replaced by some form of civilian service is under discussion at government level.

This change of attitudes is partly the result of developments in international relations, which increasingly cast doubt on the necessity and acceptability of a military solution to problems.

EXAM TIP

This type of discussion question in activity 3 sometimes occurs in Phase C of the exam. You are asked to reach agreement or agree to differ. Because you only have four minutes to discuss the statements, you don't need to go into great detail. It is probably easier to discuss the statements in the order they are presented in.

– Deal with one statement at a time.

– Take turns to say whether you agree or disagree with the statement and offer a brief explanation.

– Reach agreement or agree to differ.

– Do the same with the next statement.

You will then be asked to report the result of your discussion to the examiners.

3 *Exam Question* Work in groups of four.

STUDENTS A and B: You are exam candidates. Discuss the statements below. You have four minutes to reach agreement or agree to differ.

– Women should do compulsory national service as well as men.
– Military service should be abolished and replaced by compulsory community work or a humanitarian civil service.
– Only people who are out of work should be obliged to do national service.
– It is up to each individual citizen to decide how and when he or she should serve his or her nation.

STUDENTS C and D: You are examiners. Listen to Candidates A and B and use the Assessment grid on page 99 to help you form an impression of their level.

4 Discuss the candidates' performance. Focus on both positive and negative aspects. Make suggestions for improvement.

When you are ready, change roles. Repeat activity 3 to allow STUDENTS C and D the opportunity to speak.

5 Work in groups of four or five. Read the case studies below and discuss whether the people should do their national service or not.

Paulo is 22 and is married with a baby daughter. His wife is disabled. He has had a regular job for the past three years. He is in voluntary exile in Britain because if he returns to his native Portugal, he will be imprisoned for draft-dodging.

Xavier is 26 and has just graduated as a doctor. He is single and does not have a job. He refuses to wear his uniform on humanitarian grounds. He has started a hunger strike.

Günther has just come out of prison for injuring a policeman at a football match. He wants to do his military service, but the army does not want him.

Mr X is in hiding because he has received his call-up papers. There is a civil uprising in his country and the government is using the army to fight the rebels. Mr X does not want to fight his fellow citizens.

6 In your group, decide upon a system of national service which could be applied throughout the world. If you have different views, try to reach a compromise.

Do you think young people should be able to choose to do international service under the orders of the United Nations Organisation instead of national service for their country?

UNIT
11

Time matters

Section A Listening

The aim of this section is to focus on the following.
- inferring meaning and attitude
- listening for main ideas

The exam question prepares you for Section C of the exam; it requires you to answer multiple choice questions.

1 The theme of this section is time and the human body. Answer the following questions.

- How many hours' sleep do you ideally need each night?
- Are you a *morning* or an *evening* person?
- When are you most efficient during the day? When are you least efficient?
- Would you say that your daily routine suits you?

Work in a group. Discuss your answers.

2 Work in pairs. Make a list of jobs that people do at night. How do you think working at night affects a person's life? Think about the following points.

family life   finances   health   leisure   social life   travel

Would you be prepared to do any of the jobs on your list?

STUDY TIP

When you listen to someone talking about a particular topic, you usually draw conclusions or make inferences about the person's attitude which are not necessarily clearly stated but only implied by what the person says.

Clues to attitude may be scattered throughout the discourse and listeners use all these elements to build up an overall impression. For example, someone talking about his or her job may mention many positive aspects and minimise the negative ones. It is therefore possible to infer that the person likes his or her job, even if they have not actually said so.

3 You are going to hear two people who work at night talking about their jobs and how night work affects their lives.

Listen to the recording. Decide what the people's jobs are and if they have adapted satisfactorily to night work.

4 With your partner, discuss your answers to the following questions about the speakers in activity 3.

- Are they married or single?
- Why did they choose their jobs?
- Are there any advantages in working at night?
- What are the main disadvantages?
- Would they like to change jobs?
- How does their work affect their social life?

Listen to the recording again and check your answers.

5 You are going to hear two people explaining how specific time changes affect them.

📼 🎧 Listen to the recording. What situations are the speakers talking about?

Listen to the recording again. Note down how the speakers were affected and how long it took them to adapt and/or recover.

Check your notes with your partner. Have you ever experienced these time changes? If so, tell your partner about your experiences.

6 You are going to hear an expert talking about human biological rhythms. She mentions the following points.

– the influence of the sun and the moon
– genetic research and new drugs
– the biological clock
– disturbed biorhythms and health problems
– the advantages of putting the clocks forward in northern countries
– what body organs regulate our body rhythms

Now read the Exam question in activity 7 carefully. In answer to which questions do you think she mentions the above points?

EXAM TIP

Multiple choice questions are usually found in Section C of the exam. There are usually six or seven multiple choice questions, each one having four optional answers. Only one answer is correct.

The questions normally follow the order of information in the recording, so if you follow the questions as you listen, this will help you identify the answers.

Because the recording is quite long – approximately four minutes – don't try and answer all the questions during the first listening.

– Listen to the whole recording for general meaning and to identify the passages which concern the questions.
– Eliminate the most obvious wrong answers.
– Answer the most obvious questions.
– Listen again and answer the remaining questions.

7 ⌨ 📻 *Exam Question*   You will hear an interview between a radio presenter and a biologist who studies human biological rhythms. Answer the questions by choosing the best answer A, B, C or D. You will hear this piece twice.

1 How do most people feel about putting the clocks forward?
   A they are indifferent
   B they disapprove
   C they find it hard to adapt
   D they approve

2 What governs most human biological functions?
   A the interaction of the sun and the moon
   B the length of day
   C the circadian rhythms
   D the body temperature

1	
2	
3	
4	
5	
6	

3 When are human biological rhythms disturbed?
   A when we put the clocks forward
   B whenever the biological clock does not match the environment
   C when we do shift work
   D when we are ill

4 Why is the study of biorhythms useful to medicine?
   A it can help prevent heart attacks
   B it can help researchers develop new drugs
   C doctors can treat disturbed sleep patterns
   D doctors can choose the best time of day to operate on or administer drugs to patients

5 How does the increase in daylight affect people?
   A it contributes to their general well-being and efficiency
   B it makes people feel happier
   C people who work get more leisure time in the evenings
   D it helps prevent a number of diseases

6 What is the main reason for changing the clocks?
   A social
   B medical
   C economic
   D biological

8 Do the clocks change to summer time in your country? If so, why?

Section B Speaking

The aim of this section is to focus on the following.
– matching cartoons to captions
– discussing and drawing conclusions

The exam question prepares you for Phase C of the exam; it requires you to match two parts of sentences.

1 Read the following passage and answer the questions.

> ### HOW WELL DO YOU MANAGE YOUR TIME?
>
> Managing time has become a major preoccupation in our high-speed modern society. More and more people follow Time Management courses to help them improve their efficiency and keep up with the pace of daily life.
>
> **At work or studies:**
> – Are you always on time for appointments, lessons or work?
> – Do you tend to do the quick, easy and enjoyable things first and put off things that are unpleasant?
> – Do you tend to jump around from task to task and leave things unfinished?
> – Do you fix yourself objectives and priorities and keep to them?
> – Are you self-disciplined?
> – Are you easily distracted?
> – Do you often feel pressed for time and overloaded with work?
>
> **In your life in general:**
> – Do you ever feel under stress because you have too many things to do at once?
> – Do you do something enjoyable every day?
> – Do you have enough leisure time?
> – Do you have clear, long-term personal objectives or do you live from one day to the next?
> – Are you as careful with your time as you are with your money?
> – Finally, would you say that you are in control of your time and work, or do they control you?

2 Work in groups of three or four. Discuss your answers to the questions in activity 1. Decide who would benefit from a Time Management course. Make a list of things you could do to improve the way you organise your time. How do you think a Time Management course would benefit you?

3 🔑 **Work in pairs. Match the captions with the cartoons below. There are two extra captions.**

1 'And how was *your* day?'
2 Be master of your own time.
3 We cannot stop the passage of time.
4 Don't let yourself be distracted by unimportant matters.
5 Time saved is money saved.
6 Since he's been working under pressure of time, he seems to be only a shadow of his former self.
7 Each day you should do something that you enjoy.
8 Ease up and rely more on management delegation.

4 Work with another pair of students. Discuss the ideas the cartoons express. Which ones do you agree with? For the extra captions which have no cartoon pictures, can you imagine a suitable picture?

EXAM TIP

In Phase C of the exam, the problem solving task may be in a variety of different forms. It may require ranking, which is putting things in order of importance, sequencing, which is putting things in the right order, or matching, which involves putting the two parts of a sentence together, or putting a heading or caption with a picture. This is the part of the exam which is the least predictable. Don't forget that it is your skills of evaluation and negotiation in English that are being tested. It is how you do the task which is important, not whether you achieve it successfully. The examiners are checking your ability to speak, not other skills you may or may not have.

5 ☎ **With your partner, reach agreement or agree to differ on the best way of combining the two parts of the sentences below.**

Take time to ...	
Take time to work;	it is the road to happiness.
Take time to play;	it is the source of power.
Take time to think;	it is the joy of life.
Take time to read;	it is the price of success.
Take time to be friendly;	it is the music of the soul.
Take time to love;	it is the secret of perpetual youth.
Take time to laugh;	it is the fountain of wisdom.

6 *Exam question* Work in groups of four. Do not work with the partner you worked with in activity 5.

STUDENTS A and B: You are exam candidates. Reach agreement or agree to differ on the best way of combining the two parts of the sentences in activity 5.
STUDENTS C and D: You are examiners. Listen to candidates A and B and use the Assessment grid on page 99 to help you form an impression of their level.

7 Repeat activity 6 to allow STUDENTS C and D the opportunity to speak. Change roles.

8 Look at the original sentences on page 129 with your partner. Find out if you chose the same combinations. Which do you agree with? Which do you disagree with?

12

Town and country

Section A Listening

The aim of this section is to focus on the following.

– listening for specific information

The first exam question prepares you for Section B of the exam; it gives you one opportunity only to complete a chart with specific information from a recording. The second exam question also prepares you for Section B; it gives you one opportunity only to label a map with specific information from a recording.

1 Work in pairs. Which are the most popular towns or regions to visit in your country? Make a list of the features which attract tourists there.

2 The Cotswolds is a region in England which is very popular with tourists. Look at the photos below of villages in the Cotswolds. What do you think attracts so many people? Would you like to visit these places?

3 Read the following description of the Cotswolds. Find out what attracts tourists there. Compare the ideas you mentioned in activity 2 with what the passage says.

The Cotswolds are the very picture of perfect England. The centuries-old houses are part of the national consciousness. They, and the placid sheep grazing on the gentle slopes of the Windrush and Evenlode valleys, represent a dream of rural England we all want to share. And that's the difficulty. Pretty Bourton-on-the-Water and Burford are swamped by coach parties and Bibury, a perfect English village, can sometimes be a slow-moving traffic jam. Yet five miles away the tiny hamlet of Icomb, with the Norman church of St Mary the Virgin but no pub or shop, is enveloped in silence, while the market towns of Northleach and Moreton-in-the-Marsh lie between the extremes, with locals going about their everyday business largely untroubled by tourism.

The pale limestone hills of the Cotswolds extend for 55 miles across Gloucestershire into Oxfordshire, Wiltshire and Worcestershire. In parts the range is 30 miles wide and its highest point, just south of Cheltenham, is just over 1,000 feet.

It's full of fascinating places like Sudeley Castle and Snowshill Manor, and there's plenty for the kids too at the Cotswold Wildlife Park.

With a good map, you can abandon the main roads and follow the narrow green lanes which will reveal wonderful views of the countryside and lead you to uncrowded pubs at country cross-roads. The landscape is laced with well-marked footpaths, ancient ways followed for centuries by salt traders, pack horses and pilgrims. Enthusiastic walkers can follow the Cotswold Way which runs for 107 miles from Bath to Chipping Camden.

4 📼 🔊 *Exam Question* You will hear a tourist asking for information about a variety of places to visit in the Cotswolds. As you listen, fill in the information for items 1-10. Listen carefully as you will hear this piece once only.

Sudeley Castle	open from	1 [ ]	to 2 [ ]
	entrance fee	3 [ ]	for adults,
		4 [ ]	for children
Snowshill Manor	What is it?	5 [ ]	
	Open until	6 [ ]	
Lygon Arms	Where is it?	7 [ ]	
	Cost for weekend	8 [ ]	
	Extra costs	9 [ ]	
	Telephone	10 [ ]	

5 🗀 ⇥ *Exam Question*   You will hear someone in a tourist office explaining where to go and what to see in the Cotswolds. On the map, write down what you can see or visit in the various places. The places are numbered in the order in which they are mentioned. Listen carefully as you will hear this piece once only.

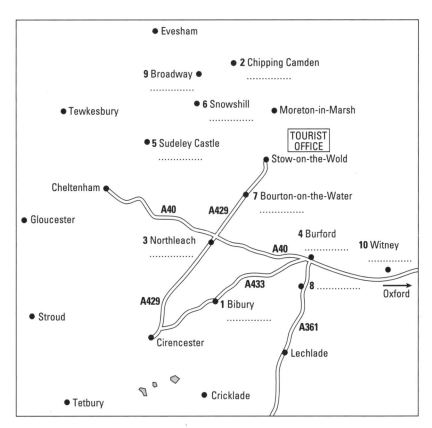

6 With your partner, make a list of interesting things to do and see in the popular towns and regions which you discussed in activity 1.

Do you think the number of tourists visiting these places creates a serious problem? What can be done about this?

Section B Speaking

The aim of this section is to focus on the following.

- ranking features of a town
- commenting on a description of a city and giving personal opinions

The exam question prepares you for Phase B of the exam; it requires you to describe and draw a picture from a spoken description.

1 Which of the following features do you consider to be important for life in the city?

> accessibility   beautiful buildings   cheap public transport
> cycle lanes   good entertainment   good restaurants   good schools
> lots of young people   museums and galleries   parks and trees
> pleasant climate   safe streets   shops   sports facilities   suitable size
> traffic control

Choose ten features and number them in order of importance from 1 (not very important) to 10 (very important).

2 Work in pairs. Talk about the features you chose in activity 1. Define the features you chose according to your own requirements and expectations. What do you think of your partner's choice and order of the features? Try to reach agreement on a list.

3 With your partner, decide if you would like to live in the city in the photo below. What would be the advantages and disadvantages? Make a list.

4 Read the article about the futurist city of Arcosanti, in Arizona, USA, which you can see in the photo on the previous page.

About seventy miles north of Phoenix, off Interstate 17, past a sad collection of buildings that make up a place called Cordes Junction, and then a couple of miles along a dirt road is Arcosanti, the city of the future. There's a 'drive slowly' sign, but you don't need telling – the road is potholed and in places scrapes the bottom of your car.

Arcosanti is the architect Paolo Soleri's version of how future generations might live: in compact, high density, hive-like structures where there will be no need for cars or even public transport; distances will be short with moving pavements to convey people around. The city will, of course, be ecologically sound, big on solar power and recycling. Above all, it will be surrounded by vast areas of farmland and wilderness. This is not precisely what you find at Arcosanti.

What you do find is a complex, fussy tangle of structures, mostly made of concrete. There is one solid, chunky, more or less conventional-looking block of a building that houses a restaurant, bakery and gallery but stretching away from it, reaching out across the desert, is a series of arches – some free-standing, some like the mouths of caves, some filled in with windows and doors. Elsewhere the shapes are those of simple building blocks: the square, the cube, the circle, the hemisphere.

It looks wild and weird, but above all looks unfinished – as indeed it is. Arcosanti is a work in progress, and progress is slow. After 20 years only 3 per cent is finished. It has a rough, temporary look about it, part stage set, part camp site, a visual style somewhere between Woodstock and *Mad Max*.

Arcosanti is not a pretty place. It has the feel of a Sixties university campus out of term – barren and windswept, a place that people are passing through and only provisionally claiming as their own.

It is the soaring ambition of Arcosanti which makes its current state so pitiable. Envisaged as a city for 5,000 people, it currently holds about 50. Extraordinarily over-endowed with stages and performance spaces, it is lacking in other urban necessities, such as clothes stores, supermarkets, newsagents.

And yet, and yet … Soleri does seem to be addressing a very real problem. America has a lot of space and is proud of the fact, but every day it has a bit less. Current architectural thinking aims to give everyone their own home on a fenced patch of land. But a growing population and an active building industry suggest that sooner or later, even America is in danger of becoming one giant continuous suburb.

There is some crucial opposition at stake here. Do we try to live happily in close proximity with our neighbours, or do we put as much distance as possible between them and ourselves – a distance that inevitably is not going to be so very great, and which needs to be reinforced with high walls, hedges, fences, barbed wire and security systems?

Paolo Soleri wants to keep a distinction between town and country. If people can tolerate each other's presence on a day-to-day basis, then there will still be vast wildernesses for them to retreat to. If people insist on turning the wilderness into their own backyard, there will be nowhere for them to get away to, and any tiny pockets of wilderness that are preserved will be no more than highly regulated theme parks.

Geoff Nicholson,
The Independent on Sunday 14 August 1994

Discuss the following questions with your partner.

- Does the writer create a positive or negative image of Arcosanti? Can you explain why?
- Does Paolo Soleri's vision of how future generations might live appeal to you?
- What features will the city of the future have? Which of these features appeal to you?
- Does the writer think it will look better when it's finished? Do you?
- Can you answer the writer's question in the penultimate paragraph?
- Would you like to live there? Would the writer? Would you like to visit Arcosanti?

The type of task in activity 6 is likely to be found in Phase B of the interview; it involves a kind of picture dictation. It can involve maps and plans of rooms or houses. It is important to remember that the task is not designed to test the listening skills of the candidate who is taking the dictation. He or she will not be penalised for not positioning the objects correctly. It is the speaking ability of the candidate giving the dictation which is being tested.

5 *Exam Question* Work in pairs. You are going to describe and draw a picture. You have about a minute to do this. Please do not show your pictures to each other.

STUDENT A: Turn to page 95.
STUDENT B: Turn to page 96.

6 Repeat activity 6 to allow Student B the opportunity to speak. Change roles.

STUDENT A: Turn to page 97.
STUDENT B: Turn to page 98.

7 **Work in groups of three or four. Which of these quotations do you agree with?**

> I have an affection for a great city. I feel safe in the neighbourhood of man, and enjoy the sweet security of the streets.
> *Longfellow, 1857*
>
> There is no solitude in the world like that of the big city.
> *Kathleen Norris*
>
> The difference between town and country is mostly the view.
> *Nan Fairbrother*
>
> Lovers of the town have been content to say they loved it. They do not brag about its uplifting qualities. They have none of the infernal smugness which makes the lover of the country insupportable.
> *Agnes Repplier, 1931*

Can you write a quotation which shows how you feel about life in the town and in the country?

Role cards and extra material

Unit 2 Activity 7

Examiner's role card: UK version

You are the examiner. Here are additional questions to ask the candidates:

Candidate A, could you tell Candidate B about what it's like to live in … ?

Candidate B, does that sound like the sort of place you'd like to live in or visit?

Candidate B, could you now tell Candidate A about where you live?

Both of you come from places that are (very) different from England.

- Is there anything you particularly like or don't like about England?
- How long are you staying here?
- How do you plan to use your English in your future life?
- What exactly do you want to do in the future?

Examiner's role card: international version

You are the examiner. Here are some additional questions to ask the candidates:

Now can you ask each other why you're learning English and talk about your plans for the future?

Well, you both live here in … . What would you say are the good things about living in … ? Are there any disadvantages?

- How do you both travel to school/college?
- What is the best means of transport round here?
- What interesting places are there to visit here?
- Where are the best places to stay/eat?

Unit 3, Activity 6 Candidate A

Candidate A: Describe the picture to Candidate B. Please do not show your picture to Candidate B.

Unit 3, Activity 6, Candidate B

Candidate B: Describe the picture to Candidate A. Please do not show your picture to Candidate A.

Unit 5, Activity 7, Candidate A

Candidate A: Choose two photos and describe them as fully as possible so that Candidate B can identify them. You have about a minute to do this.

Unit 5, Activity 7, Candidate B

Candidate B: Listen to Candidate A describing two of these photos and decide which he/she is describing. If you are uncertain after he/she has finished, you may ask him/her questions to help you identify the photos. Otherwise, say what helped you recognise the photos.

Unit 5, Activity 8, Candidate A

Candidate A: Listen to Candidate B describing two of these photos and decide which he/she is describing. If you are uncertain after he/she has finished, you may ask him/her questions to help you identify the photos. Otherwise, say what helped you recognise the photos.

Unit 5, Activity 8, Candidate B

Candidate B: Choose two photos and describe them as fully as possible so that Candidate A can identify them. You have about a minute to do this.

Unit 6, Activity 5, Candidate B

Candidate B: Describe the photo below to Candidate C. Talk about the market and what kind of food you get there. Please do not show your photo to Candidate C.

Unit 6, Activity 5, Candidate C

Candidate C: Candidate B will describe a photo. Your photo is similar but not the same. Listen carefully and say two things which are the same in your photo and two things which are different. Please do not show your photo to Candidate B.

Unit 6, Activity 6, Candidate A

Candidate A: Describe the photo below to Candidate B. Talk about the supermarket and what kind of food you get there. Please do not show your photo to Candidate B.

Unit 6, Activity 6, Candidate B

Candidate B: Candidate A will describe a photo. Your photo is similar but not the same. Listen carefully and say two things which are the same in your photo and two things which are different. Please do not show your photo to Candidate A.

Unit 12, Activity 5, Candidate A

Candidate A: Describe the position of the facilities in the picture as clearly as possible so that Candidate B can draw a plan of where they should be. You have about one minute to do this. Please do not show your picture to Candidate B.

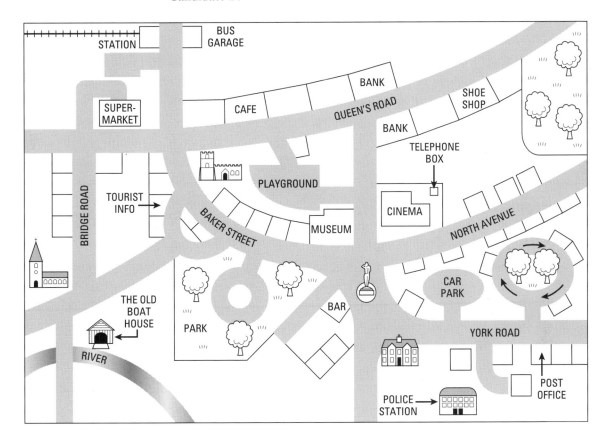

Unit 12, Activity 5, Candidate B

Candidate B: Listen to Candidate A and draw the facilities in the position he/she describes on your plan.

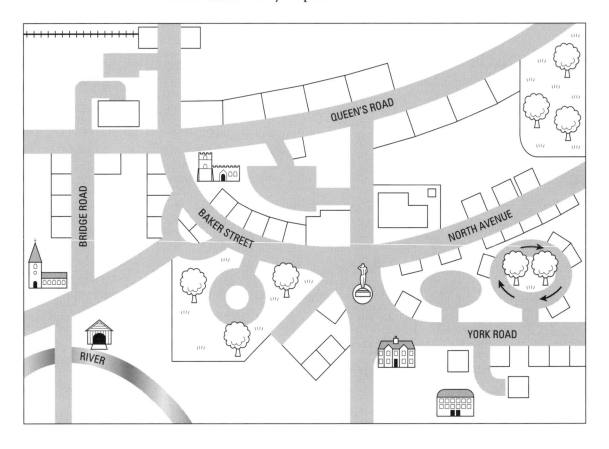

Unit 12, Activity 6, Candidate A

Candidate A: Listen to Candidate B and draw the facilities in the position
he/she describes on your plan.

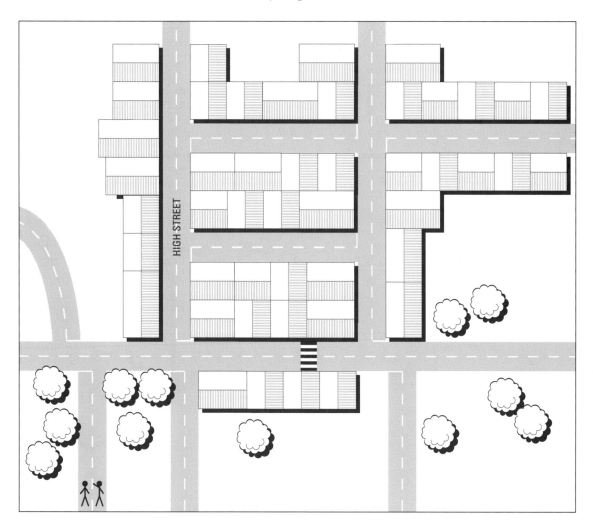

Unit 12, Activity 6, Candidate B

Candidate B: Describe the position of the facilities in the picture as clearly as possible so that Candidate A can draw a plan of where they should be. You have about one minute to do this. Please do not show your picture to Candidate A.

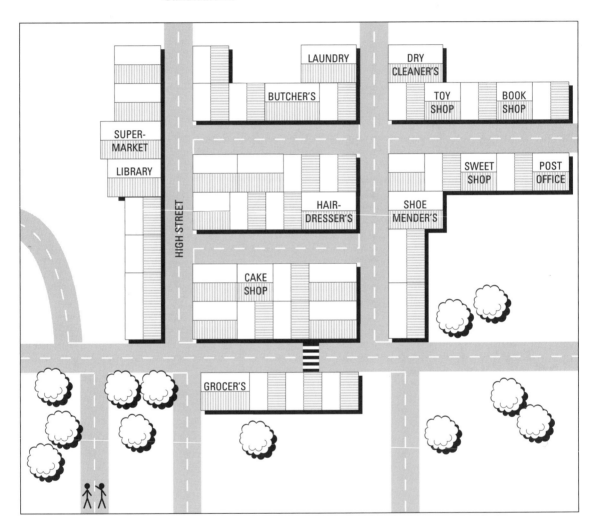

Assessment grid

	Fluency	Accuracy	Pronunciation	Task achievement	Interactive communication
7–8	Coherent spoken interaction with good speed and rhythm. Few intrusive hesitations.	Evidence of a wide range of structures and vocabulary. Errors minimal in number and gravity.	Little L1 accent/L1 accent not obtrusive. Good mastery of English pronunciation features.	The tasks are dealt with fully and effectively. The language is appropriate to each task.	Contributes fully and effectively throughout the interaction.
5–6	Occasional but noticeable hesitations, but not such as to strain the listener or impede communication.	Evidence of a good range of structures and vocabulary. Errors few in number and minor in gravity. These errors do not impede communication.	Noticeable L1 accent having minor difficulties with some pronunciation features. These do not strain the listener or impede communication.	The tasks are mostly dealt with effectively but with minor inadequacies of execution or language.	Contributes with ease for most of the interaction, with only occasional and minor difficulties.
3–4	Fairly frequent and noticeable hesitations. Communication is achieved but strains the listener at times.	Fairly frequent errors and evidence of restricted range of structures and/or vocabulary. These do not prevent communication of the essential message.	Obvious L1 pronunciation features with major defects. These may strain the listener and/or make comprehension of detail difficult.	One or more of the tasks are dealt with in a limited manner. The language is often inappropriate. Redirection may have been required at times.	Contributes effectively for some of the interaction, but fairly frequent difficulties.
1–2	Disconnected speech and/or frequent hesitations impede communication and strain the listener.	Frequent basic errors and limited range of structures and/or vocabulary impede communication and strain the listener.	Heavy L1 pronunciation and widespread difficulties with English features impede communication of the message and strain the listener.	Inadequate attempts at the tasks using little appropriate language. Requires major redirection or assistance.	Difficulty in maintaining contributions throughout. May respond to simple or structured interaction but obvious limitations in freer situations.

0   Sample of language inadequate for assessment (even after prompting by the interlocutor).

Answer sheet for **Paper 4 Listening**

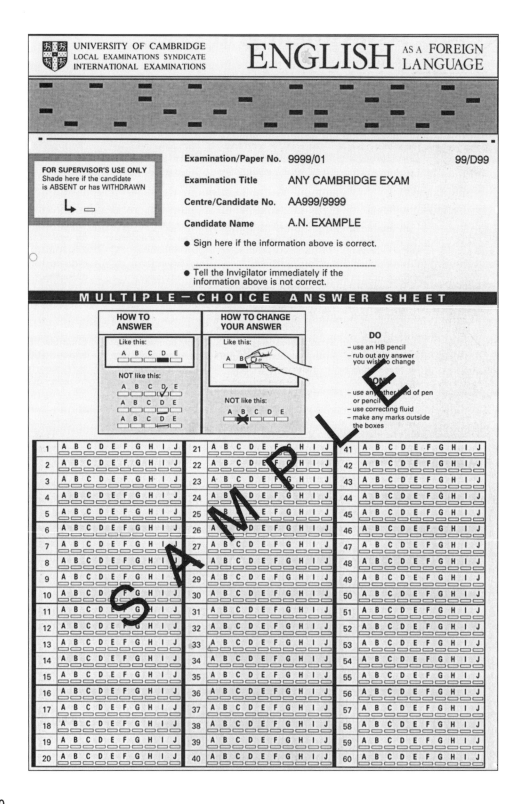

Tapescript

Unit I Foundation unit, Section A Listening

1 A: Well, the listening paper for CAE is on tape, and it includes all the time needed to read the questions, write the answers and transfer them to the answer sheet, which is called the OMR. So when you're running the exam, you don't have to keep stopping the tape to give the candidates time to complete their answers. The whole exam takes about 30 minutes in all. Now, there are three basic question types: multiple choice, gap fill and matching techniques. The texts come from a number of different sources, such as radio broadcasts and announcements, conversations and discussions, speeches, talks and lectures and what we call vox pop interviews, which are little extracts from interviews with people in the street. There are four sections, A, B, C and D and there'll be between 40 and 50 questions or items. Sections A, C and D are heard twice and Section B is heard only once. The text type in Section A is usually a monologue, in Section B a short descriptive passage, in Section C a dialogue or discussion and in Section D a series of short extracts lasting about 10–30 seconds. The skills tested are extracting main information, understanding gist or general impression, the attitudes and points of view of the speakers and identifying the speakers or source or nature of what they're listening to. The instructions on the question paper and the tape will be the same and the aim is to create a context for the listening passage and to give the students help in answering the questions. I think that's everything, but please ask questions if you have any.

B: How long should we allow candidates for completing the answer sheet at the end of the exam?

A: The tape specifies that there'll be a short pause. Allow a minute or two, but no longer.

C: Should we intervene at all during the exam? For instance, to repeat certain instructions if some candidates look puzzled?

A: That's very difficult. No, the material we use has been pretested and any confusion should have been ironed out long before you use it in the exam. No, I'm afraid that if someone looks confused, it's their English which isn't up to scratch, not the instructions.

4 Extract 1
There's a short gap between each section for you to complete your answers, and in addition, you will have approximately two minutes at the end of Section D to allow you to check your work.

Extract 2
Section A. You will hear a woman calling the Tourist Information Office in a town called Halifax where she is organising a meeting. She wants to book lunch and dinner at different restaurants and she wants to find out what they can offer. For questions 1 to 12 tick the boxes or put in the prices while you are listening to the conversation. Some of the boxes have been filled in for you and you will find it necessary to leave some boxes blank. You will hear the piece twice.

Extract 3
A: So how did it go Chantal?
B: Oh, I don't know, I didn't feel very happy about it.
A: Oh, I'm sorry. What went wrong?
B: Well, I found the instructions very confusing, and so long, and when I got the paper I just didn't know where to look. There were a couple of questions which I just had to guess, and there were a few others which I wasn't sure about.

Extract 4
C: Can I have your ticket, sir? And your passport? Ah, I'm sorry sir but I'm afraid your flight is fully booked.
D: But that's not possible. I confirmed the booking a few days ago.
C: I'm very sorry sir, but the flight has been overbooked, but we can offer you a place on a later flight. There's one at 16.30.
D: But this is outrageous. You can't do this. I've

got to get on that flight. I booked the ticket months ago, and I reconfirmed last week.

C: It's just that you're a little late sir. You've only left half an hour before the plane leaves.

D: I was stuck in a traffic jam! Now you listen to me …

Extract 5

E: Well, that's over.

F: Yes, I can't say I enjoy it very much. Watching all those poor kids straining to understand the passages. They seem to speak very quickly.

E: Well it's normal speed actually, and I reckon if they're carefully prepared for it, it shouldn't be too difficult. I mean, most of them are ready for the exam as far as their language competence is concerned.

F: I suppose so. It's just the circumstances of the exam which are tough. I'm glad I've done all my exams.

Unit I Foundation unit, Section B Speaking

1 Ex: Hello, my name's Steve Chadwick and this is my colleague, Reanna Williams.

P and A: Hello.

Ex: And your names are?

P: Patrick

A: Alessandro.

Ex: Do the two of you know each other?

P: Yes. We have been together in the same class.

A: Should I introduce him? Or should …

Ex: Yes, if you like, Alessandro, you could tell us a little bit about Patrick.

A: He is Patrick. He comes from Switzerland and he is 26 years old. And he graduated last December in economics. And after this course he will look for a job in his country.

Ex: Can you tell us something about how Patrick is in the class?

A: Umm. The teacher said, or usually says that he is a bit demanding and … yeah, because he he likes er he likes er demanding or strange questions or very difficult questions and sometimes the teacher er is not in a position to under … to answer all the questions he …

Ex: Yeah, so he's a difficult student. Do you

think that's true?

P: Maybe. I heard this say once.

Ex: From a student or a teacher?

P: No, from a teacher.

Ex: Good. Now, Patrick, could you tell us a little bit about Alessandro?

P: Yes, his name is Alessandro. He is coming from Switzerland as well but not from the German but, from the Italian part. He is studying economics as well, but in St Gallen and he is now, I think, in the middle of his studies and he will have it will take him another two years to graduate. And I think he is here now because he would like to work once in an English country and for this he has to prove that he has a certain level of English and he will achieve this here in this school, I hope so.

Ex: You think he's learnt a lot of English?

P: Yeah, I think so really, because he was quite quiet in the beginning and now he became more and more lively. And he … yeah he can express himself now properly, I would say.

Ex: Good, good. And could you perhaps, could you tell us a little bit about how Alessandro spends his spare time, can you?

P: His spare time. I think he is usually, first he goes to the learning centre … he is reading the newspaper and doing the homework or something like this. And then he goes quite often jogging or sometimes I heard that he is er that he went swimming or something like this. He spends a lot of time doing sport on the whole. And in the evening, as everybody he's a pub …

Ex: Every night? Is that fair?

A: Yes, almost every night. No, I like pubs and I like this habit to go to the pub in the evening and to have beers and nuts and crisps and to chat a bit …

4 Ex: In the next part of the test I'm going to give each of you a picture to look at. Please do not show your pictures to each other.

Now, your pictures are similar but they are not the same. And I'd like you, Samantha, to describe your picture fully to Marena. Talk about the room and the people who might live there. You have about a minute for this.

And I'd like you, please, Marena, to listen carefully and then tell us briefly two things which are the same in your picture and two things which are different. Here is some spare paper if you'd like to make notes.

M: Notes. Thank you.

S: OK. My picture is showing a dining room. There are some sofa and on the ground there is a carpet, a big carpet and some toys and they're in a mess. And there are a lot of pillow everywhere in the room and also flowers, dried flowers, and bottles of alcohol. And then there are two bookshelves with some books in them and three pictures on the wall. There is a fireplace, probably an artificial fireplace. And there is also these … with some fruit inside. And on the fireplace there are three candles, a picture of a baby and some pencils. There is also a television. And the newspaper on the armchair …

Ex: Thank you. Now, Marena, I'd like you to say very briefly how your picture is different and how it is the same as Samantha's.

M: I dunno I've got some sitting room but there is … in it as well, and chairs. I just think that there are different people living in my kind of room because I think it's it's a cosy room with a ball of wool and I think it's like old people living there. There is no television – there is a fireplace but I think there is stove in it umm there are no toys, but there are books like yours … so I think they like reading.

Ex: That's fine. Would you like to compare your two pictures?

M: It looks quite like – I thought that this could be more for younger people or …

S: A family with a baby I think.

M: Yeah, yeah and I don't think your are even older elder people.

S: An old woman probably because she's working with her ball of wool, yeah …

M: and a cup of tea

S: and biscuits

Ex: OK thanks. Can I collect the pictures back please?

6 Ex: Now, I'd like you both to look at this picture. Talk about it and decide what kind of person it represents. Talk about his possible age, sex, nationality and personality. Try also to guess what the purpose of the picture is, who it is aimed at and how effective you think it is. And you have three or four minutes to do this.

A: Shall we start with the nationality? Because …

P: Yes. This is obvious, I think.

A: No, it's not so obvious. It could be either an English or a German, I think, because there is a big potato and it represents – it could be both of them.

P: Yeah. At least this is not for us to describe it is not a usual person so this is a person represented by a potato.

A: Yes – sure.

P: and …

A: and the roots the roots represent the legs and the arms.

P: Yeah, and what is in front of his feet? Do you see this? There are french fries and the burger …

A: French fries on the ground and the pack, burger package, and, er …

P: There's a lot of junk food, I think really, you see here Coke, another packet of crisps or something like this.

A: Yeah, yeah

P: I think this is a person who might have died in front of the TV because he was, I know, maybe overjunked or – there are so many videos here. I really I think maybe this should express the sickness of our civilisation or culture.

A: I don't completely agree, I think it's a representation of of modern life and modern habits. So fast foods and TV and video cassettes, video tapes and, yeah, it's a good representation of modern life, I think. I think it's a bit excessive to say that he died – because of this…

P: I don't know, but, he looks so …, he doesn't look very comfortable – I would say – look his eyes – I don't know.

A: He has got also a bit of a belly.

P: Too much beer maybe.

A: too much beer … hamburgers.

P: and here is the TV, you know. I think maybe he never – you know – I think he can control everything out from his armchair, he is all the day in his chair. He has here his remote control – to change or switch the programmes and to eat, he doesn't have to move anymore.

A: He doesn't have to move yeah he doesn't need it because …

P: Sorry, yes …?

A: You can see also food on the ground, and a cup of tea, some plates …

P: You know I think maybe …

A: and a bowl …

P: this should representative as well that he doesn't cook anymore. He just goes around the corner maybe or he orders his food by telephone.

A: But that's it. That's why I say it's a representation of modern life. Also an open bag – it is the typical bag for pizza, when you receive the pizza delivered from –

P: Yeah, that's true …

Unit 2 Different backgrounds, Section A Listening

3 Interview 1

I: Sharon Harper, now you're a Canadian and you live in Helsinki.

SH: That's right.

I: Well, can you tell me why did you come to Finland?

SH: Well I came to Finland – it was right after I finished university in Toronto where I studied literature – I always wanted to be a journalist – and the reason I came to Finland was just for a summer job.

I: Oh really?

SH: Yes – um – some friends of my parents were offering a small summer job, you know for – in Helsinki and I thought well that would be an interesting experience. I must have really liked it because I've lived in Helsinki now for nine years. I'm a foreign correspondent for a business magazine and I really like Finland. I guess originally the attraction was, you know Finland is off the beaten track – a little less obvious than say going to Paris or Rome and that makes it somewhat exotic and not many Americans – some don't even know Finland exists, of course. They don't seem to come here and it's so beautiful, they don't know how beautiful it is.

I: I'm sure. What do you think the differences are really between life in Canada and in Finland?

SH: Well, I suppose there is quite a big cultural difference. That would apply really between any European country and America, I suppose. But Finland has a very old and rich culture which they want to preserve – that beautiful part of Helsinki which has been preserved as an original Finnish village with all the wooden buildings, the sloping roofs for the snow. It's quite beautiful. Now North America had a culture which I suppose was the culture of the native Americans but that was largely destroyed by the Europeans – so, to that extent America's a very new country and I love the sense of history that the Finns have as a nation and they can look back on. But at the same time they're very outward looking. That's a strange thing. At the same time they love their history but they're more outward looking than Americans I would say.

I: That's interesting.

SH: Yeah, I think that Americans and Canadians too are egocentric, inward looking, they're not very concerned with life outside their continent. That's a fault really, isn't it?

I: I suppose so, yes.

SH: There are some things – in some ways Finland resembles Canada. The physical appearance of it, the – the woods, and rock, Northern Ontario particularly we get away from the cities and the water, that does remind me of home. I like that side of it, yeah.

I: So what would you say really were the positive aspects of Finland?

SH: Well, there's always the sauna. Though I confess I wouldn't be too keen on the rolling in the snow after the sauna which I guess Finns are keen on. But it's certainly a wonderful invention, isn't it? You feel great after you've had a sauna. The Finns like the simple pleasures in life which – that appeals to me of course too. I like trekking in the forests and mushroom picking and all the water sports are wonderful because the water's so pure and clear – boating, swimming.

I: What about the people?

SH: Well the people are – they're very genuine. Now, there's a lot of talk about how friendly Americans are but you know – that 'have a nice day', 'have a nice day' with the smile – there's a lot of phoniness behind that you know – you look in the eyes they're a bit cold – they'll put on that surface charm and you feel if a Finn appears to like you and smiles at you, then it's genuine, it's true.

I: So what would you say were the negative aspects of Finland?

SH: Well, the Finnish people can be blunt to the point of rudeness sometimes and I did say I know, that Americans could be superficial but, on the other hand, sometimes you feel the Finns have no social charm at all. They have no phrase for excuse me, for instance, (really?) no, so it takes you a while to get used to the fact that that's just the way they are and they don't mean to be rude. That's just a blunt quality to the Finnish nature. And of course, if you want negative aspects, there is that long, dark winter. Which at first I found very depressing. I'm getting used to it now but it can be really depressing. I know that in Canada we have the cold and it snows a lot but many many days you have beautiful sunlight (yeah) all the main part of the day. So just to have endless night. It can be very soul destroying when you're not used to it.

I: So what do you really miss about Canada then?

SH: Well, I think primarily my family and friends, you know, I go back once a year and I visit you know the parents and brothers and sisters and all their family, their children. Getting to know them as they grow, I think, is what you miss. You just see them from one year to the next. And I love those hot Canadian summers, not so much in Toronto but getting out of Toronto, the cottage area. Lovely hot weather. And the beautiful colour in the trees in the autumn, the wonderful sugar maples and elm trees turn yellow, it's so beautiful in the winter, in the autumn I mean, but the winter's very much the same. Lots of snow.

I: Oh well, thank you Sharon. That's really very interesting.

SH: Not at all.

Interview 2

I: Stephen Wareham, you're from Britain.

SW: Yep.

I: So why're you living in Hungary and how did you feel about moving there?

SW: Umm. Why am I living in Hungary? Well my wife's Hungarian so umm I moved to Budapest because she found it rather difficult really to adapt to obviously what is a very different life in England. Umm, so when we when I came to Hungary it was, it was a very exciting time actually, a lot was changing, you know, but um but obviously it felt strange, for me umm but you know obviously well you get used to anything as time you know has gone on I've become sort of more comfortable here. I'm I'm a freelance food and wine writer so it's a very interesting time that way obviously because you know the wines if I were going to France it wouldn't be so interesting with you know because everything's been discovered about French wines but there's so much you know more obviously with Hungarian wines. So, umm I want to get more involved with sort of import exports of you know different sort of foodstuffs to Hungary.

I: Right, yeah. Umm, so what would you say then were the difficulties of living in Hungary for you?

SW: Umm. The difficulties well, obviously the language. Umm, you know, I my Hungarian is just appalling and umm, you do feel sort of left out a bit, you know, even when friends from work or my wife's friends come to, you know, come for dinner, I can't really converse.

I: No, it's difficult.

SW: So it's yes, it is a problem.

I: Talking of that then. What's your opinion of Hungarian cuisine?

SW: Ah. Umm. Well, it's very rich, um it's a sort of peasant kind of food, you know, um pork, paprika, it's, it's quite heavy actually and umm, it's I mean obviously very different to English cooking and er the vegetables which I like sort of just you know kind of sort of with a bite with a crunch to them – are cooked to death. (Oh dear.) However, there are some very good restaurants. You know things are getting bet … and that's, you know, since I've been here things have got a lot better. You know, it'll be interesting to see how you know the food changes now that, you know, so many more different ingredients you know are readily available.

I: Yes, yes. So what would you say then were the negative aspects of life in Hungary?

SW: Well, because of, you know, the old communist system, lots of Hungarians still are a little bit negative in themselves and they find it difficult to, they lack a sort of sense of incentive in business and personal life. Umm they don't really feel that they control their own circumstances. They're still worried that you know Big Brother's looking over their shoulder and there's a lack of initiative, you know, especially when dealing with bureaucracy umm and I mean there is a point to it. Officials will often say you know no to anything that you ask them for you know for seemingly no particular reason. Umm what else, what else is there about it? Air pollution appalling appalling air pollution yeah.

I: So what would you say are the positive aspects of life in Hungary?

SW: Umm ... well, with regards to the people I mean, despite what I've just said about all their problems ... with bureaucracy and the sort of you know – they do have an extraordinary strength of character and, you know, they are a nation of survivors and umm a wonderful sense of humour, terribly dry, drole. Umm and the quality of life here is very good. The crime rate, which is appalling back home is very low here, it's not a problem. I'm not worried about, you know, kind of locking up the house and umm there's a very good cultural life, very good arts, you know generally cinema, theatre's good, umm great night life generally and what else? Public transport – marvellous, (Oh good!) marvellous.

I: So what do you miss about Britain then?

SW: Umm. Sunday newspapers – for a start. I used to love a pint in the pubs there you obviously you don't get there are bars but nothing like an English pub. And umm I'm a bri ... I was brought up in Brighton so I desperately miss the seaside.

I: Oh yes. Thank you Stephen.

SW: Thank you.

6 Int: With me now is Sean Fitzpatrick who is from Northern Ireland. Now you went to live in New York about seven years ago. Is that right?

SF: Yeah, it was about that yeah.

Int: Can you just tell me what made you decide to do that?

SF: Well I don't know really. I mean, I think I'd always wanted to live in New York. It'd always been a kind of dream of mine, you know, to go there. I was out of work at home, you know, and I scraped the money together and I just – Luckily I found some very well paid work over there as a barman, you know.

Int: I see. And is there anything about Ireland that you miss particularly?

SF: Well I miss my family, obviously, and I miss my friends you know but nothing else really.

Int: Right. So you're very happy in New York. What is it particularly about it that you like?

SF: Well, I get a lot more money over there for a start, you know which is great. And the whole lifestyle is much faster, you know it's like living life on the edge. It's great. And I have an excellent social life it's like a big party just every day of the year, you know.

Int: And is there anything else?

SF: Well, I really like the sport over there. I've really got to enjoy it, you know. In fact the best moment I've had I think since I went to America was I went to watch the New York Giants and they won the 1990 Superbowl which was absolutely fantastic. The whole place was electric. It was great.

Int: Right. Well, it all sounds very positive but is there anything about it that you don't like about New York?

SF: It's quite a dangerous place to live, you know, the crime is pretty bad. I mean I've been mugged twice already. You know and it's quite it's very unsettling. I don't like that, you know.

Int: Do you think that living in New York has changed you in anyway?

SF: I don't think so. Not really. I mean the only difference I would say is the amount of nonsense that I have to listen to from the customers in the bar, you know. They talk a lot the Americans, you know what I mean? And they talk a lot of rubbish a lot of the time, you know. But other than that, no, it's great.

Int: Good. Thanks.

Unit 3 Unusual homes, Section A Listening

2 Interview 1

About fifteen years ago my husband and I bought a windmill er near Rotterdam in Holland. Er we only paid one guilder for it – at that time people weren't really interested in living in windmills because they're draughty and there's not a lot of space and they're damp. Umm but we went ahead with our plan and we decided to restore it and make it habitable. Umm well this took about ten years to complete. Umm fortunately my husband is a teacher at a technical college and he got his students er from the woodwork and technical departments to help. Umm we er we had to we had to think very carefully about space umm because in fact there's only seven square metres of room in a windmill so what we did is we made the ground floor into a dining and kitchen area and umm the cellar became the washing machine sort of area and umm the bedroom was just sort of under the roof sort of under the hat of the mill. Umm it's been a very expensive project umm I don't think we're ever going to recoup our investment. But despite that it's umm well it's a beautiful place to live. We're surrounded by countryside, it's very peaceful, umm if you've been working all day in Rotterdam there's nothing like coming home to this tranquil surroundings. Umm there's no cars which, well it's it's wonderful on one side but on the other it means that you have to hulk your shopping two hundred metres down the dyke. But er despite all that we're we're blissfully happy.

Interview 2

I was looking for a flat to buy and hunted all over the area. It was extremely depressing because I couldn't afford anything decent. The places within my financial range were either much too small or in a dreadful neighbourhood. Then I saw this ad in the local newspaper for a house boat. I went round to see it and realised that I'd found the ideal solution to my accommodation problems. I looked around a bit before buying this boat, but there was quite a bit of choice at the time – things have changed now, lots of people have done the same as me and prices have rocketed. It was in really good condition because the previous owners had done it up really well. I only did a bit of decorating to make it suit my taste and I had one or two pieces of furniture fitted to make the kitchen and dining room more practical – you have to have things made to measure, of course, because ordinary furniture stores don't cater for boats! There are a great many advantages in living on a boat in the city. The most important to my mind, is the feeling of space. That may sound odd, because the interior is not very big and the ceilings are lower than in a normal home. But there's so much space outside – you don't have neighbours living above or below. At the most, there may be another boat moored nearby, but you don't feel cramped. And you can always move on down the river or onto the canal if you feel like a change of scenery. That's real freedom for you. The whole city is your home not just the four walls of a building!

Interview 3

Well, I suppose it's a bit unusual but I've lived in a railway carriage now for about two years. Um, it's a little scary at night because, well it's on an isolated part of the track and it's never used at all these days. And the surroundings, well they're really a little bit grim. It's not it's not really that anything's ever happened there, it's just that you you always feel a little bit insecure and a bit frightened because it's so isolated. Um, I moved originally because, well, I couldn't afford a house or a flat to rent. And railway carriages, well they're cheap to buy. Um, they're cold and draughty in the winter, I have to say. Um we've got a very small bathroom with, well only very basic plumbing. Um the kitchen's pretty good, it's quite well equipped really, I suppose. Um the children like it. I've got four children and they all like it very much because, well, there's lots of space outside for them to play and well, there's no danger of traffic or trains or anything. And originally I mean I could never have afforded a garden so they're happy about that. Er … I haven't had to do much to it at all really – not renovate anything very much, um just a little bit of decorating here and there. Er, I suppose I, well, I'll put thick curtains up before the winter and put some carpets in to keep it a little bit warmer, because it will be very cold. Er, it is a very long way from schools and er well all the services. It makes life a bit difficult. I mean I have to take two buses to take the kids to school and that's really not very easy.

6 PM: Like most children I was brought up on fairy tales and adventure stories of unexplored rain forest, Tarzan, that sort of thing. Trees were an important part of my childhood. I mean, what child hasn't dreamt of living in a tree house? I've just turned my dream into a reality, that's all. What first attracted me to this property was the garden and the remarkable variety of trees. And when we finally bought it and moved in two years ago I remember thinking that the magnificent cedar was just asking for a house to be built in it. Some people would say that I haven't grown up and still live in a fairy world. I got the idea of building in the tree when I realised that there weren't enough outbuildings and to add on a shed would have required planning permission; I really couldn't be bothered to go through all that paper work. Most of the timber came from a demolition site down the road. That was what really made me get on with it. They were pulling down an old warehouse just a few hundred yards away and they were burning everything. I thought it was a terrible waste and went down to collect it in the pick up van. So, in the end, it only cost £500 to build. The main structure didn't take long to put up. I worked on it at the weekend and in the evening when the weather was OK. I only used the house as a workshop at first. I spent so much time up there that I started taking bits and pieces from the house to make it more comfortable. Then I added on another level. Gradually it just turned into a cosy second home. The great advantage, in my view, is that you really feel you are part of nature up there. It's hard to imagine you are really right in the middle of a big industrial town. It's very safe even if sometimes it can be quite frightening when it rocks about in high winds. But at the same time it is exciting to feel part of the elements. The construction hasn't damaged the tree at all. I was careful not to use nails or restrict the growth of the cedar in any way. The only branches I cut were those which were overhanging the road; for the construction I used the main branches and sort of built around them. One great advantage which I particularly appreciated was that the local authorities haven't interfered because for the moment you don't need planning permission unless the construction is on the ground.

Unit 4 Communicating, Section A Listening

3 Extract 1
I've always been a great letter-writer. I suppose that's because I was brought up before telephones were commonplace in every home. Even now I think it's the only really civilised way of staying in contact with old friends. It's also a marvellous way of passing the time – which does pass slowly when you're retired, you know.

Extract 2
It saves me running up and down stairs to see if he's still asleep. Until we had the intercom unit fitted, I'd run up at least ten or fifteen times a day. It was exhausting!

Extract 3
Well, I don't really get on with these new gadgets but everyone in the building trade is using fax machines nowadays, so you see, I didn't have much choice. I went out and bought one. I keep it in my office at home but it's essentially a professional tool, although it does come in handy now and again at home – for booking the annual holiday, that sort of thing …

Extract 4
Before I bought it, I used to get so frustrated when the phone rang when I was in the other room and I couldn't get to it in time. Because I'm confined to a wheelchair, it's an absolute lifeline for me. I take it with me all over the house and into the garden. In fact I'm so used to having it with me that I don't feel safe if I leave it behind.

Extract 5
I spend hours chatting to my friends when I get fed up with being stuck at home. It makes my parents really mad. They say my phone calls cost them a fortune. It serves them right. They shouldn't live in such a stupid out-of-the-way place.

5 Welcome to Telecom services in Britian. This is your essential guide to telephone and fax services in Britain and we look forward to helping you use them successfully and efficiently. Wherever you're from, you can stay in touch with Telecom.

If you need to use a public telephone, you will find them in prominent locations in the streets. They are usually made of stainless steel and glass and are clearly marked. In most boxes you can use coins. The cheapest call costs ten pence, but the machine will also take fifty pence pieces and pound coins if you intend to use the phone for a long time or to call long distance.

Many phone boxes take plastic phone cards which you can buy from post offices, newsagents and corner shops for different amounts between £2 and £20. You can also use credit cards for which there is a minimum charge of 50 pence.

If you're calling abroad, the most expensive time to call someone is between 8 am and 8 pm during the week. The cheapest period is after 8 pm on weekdays and all weekend. Make sure you telephone at a time which is appropriate in the country you're calling. There may be a time difference.

You can call abroad directly from any phone by dialling 00 followed by the country and area codes and then the number. The codes for most countries and their major cities can be found in most telephone boxes. If you're calling from a private user's phone rather than a public phone box, you can place your call through the international operator on 155 and ask to be called back with the cost.

It will help if you write down the full number before you dial. Dial as carefully as you can without leaving long pauses between each digit. Your call should be connected in less than a minute. If it isn't, hang up and try again.

For more information about Telecom services, ask for our booklet which you can obtain free of charge from any Telecom shop. Thank you for calling Telecom. We hope we can help you stay in touch with your family and friends back home.

6 Extract 1

Hi, Mary. Sorry I missed you this morning. I had to rush over to the site. Trouble with the drivers. Can you cancel my appointments for this afternoon, please? Could you also tell them down in accounts that I won't be able to make it today? Try and fix something up for Thursday. If you need to contact me the site office number is 965 8849. That's 965 8849. I should be there till at least four. I'll try and stop by at the office before you leave. Thanks a lot. Bye.

Extract 2

Come along into my office. I want to have a few words with you … Now, sit there and listen carefully to what I have to say. I've had another complaint about your conduct in the classroom. Now, this isn't the first complaint I've had but I sincerely hope it will be the last – for your sake – because I'm not giving you another chance. Have I made myself absolutely clear? I shall be wanting to see your parents, of course. I'm afraid they are going to be very disappointed.

Extract 3

A: Do you know what time you'll be back this evening?
B: I'm not sure. It depends on how long the interview lasts. Oh dear, I hope things go OK. I know I can do the job, it's just getting that across to them.
A: Just relax, don't get yourself worked up. Remember, you've got to convince them that they need you and you're not going to do that if you're in a state. Have some more toast, it'll make you feel much better. Pass the jam, please. What time's your appointment?
B: 2.30.
A: Make sure you have a proper lunch. More coffee? And don't get there too early or you'll have to hang around. And there's nothing worse. You'll manage OK, I'm sure.

Extract 4

C: I'm ringing about the ad in the Weekly Herald for second hand diving equipment.
D: Yes, that's right. It hasn't gone yet.
C: Can you tell me exactly what you've got – and how much you're asking?
D: Well, there are two wet-suits, both medium adult sizes, and one set of bottles which have been checked out and certified.
C: How old are the bottles?
D: I only bought them last summer so they've hardly been used. I can show you the receipt, if you're interested.
C: When could I come and see the equipment?
D: Any evening this week would be fine.

Extract 5

E: Can I give you a lift? I'm going round via the station.
F: Oh, yes. That would be lovely.
E: Put your bag on the back seat. Er… is your door shut properly?

F: Oh, by the way, I just wanted to tell you how awful I feel about last weekend. I let everyone down, I realise that. I just couldn't face it – standing up in front of so many people – I don't know what came over me. I really am very sorry, I shouldn't have offered to do the presentations in the first place.

E: Don't worry about it. The committee understands – and anyway, Mrs Griffiths managed fine – and she thoroughly enjoyed having such a big audience for once!

F: Well, I just wanted you to know how I feel. I hardly dare show my face at another meeting. Thanks for being so understanding.

Unit 5 Unusual occupations, Section A Listening

2 I: How long have you been a lock-keeper, Mr Fielder?

Mr F: Oh dear, let me think – umm – I started when I was 25, so that means I've been at it for uh twenty-one years now. Yeah, that's it – three years on the Oxford canal and the past eighteen years here on the Reading stretch. Twenty-one years in all.

I: What did you do before you became a lock-keeper?

Mr F: I used to be an electrician. That's what I trained as.

I: Do you ever regret leaving your profession?

Mr F: Oh, no. Absolutely not. Right from the start I realised this was the one job that I would love to do. And I was right.

I: When is your most busy time of year?

Mr F: The summer months. I can easily work a ten-hour day with all the holiday traffic and the upkeep of the flower beds along the side of the lock.

3 I: Many people imagine life on the river as uneventful and easy-going. Is this right?

Mr F: Oh yes, people often ask me if I ever get bored sitting around here! In fact, I get up at six most mornings, and even in winter when there are fewer boats about, there is a lot to do, controlling the water level. When it rains hard in the night I can be up half a dozen times attending to the weir gates. No, I'm afraid the popular image of the pipe-smoking old man, leaning against the lock gate waiting for the occasional boat is far from the truth.

4 I: I believe you are the founder of Serenading Service – is that right?

PS: Yes, that's right. I started the service three years ago when I realised that British people were desperate for romance with a capital 'R'. I thought there would be a clientele for a hired serenader.

I: How did you begin your career as a singer?

PS: I started singing as a choirboy and at the age of ten I was chosen to sing alongside Placido Domingo at a charity do. That's what really got me started on a musical career. I went on to study music and then I joined an Opera company.

5 I: Where did the idea of serenading come from?

PS: From my studies of Renaissance music, and, of course, opera, which is full of serenades. On the continent, especially in Spain and Italy where it still thrives, it is a traditional romantic experience. Over the centuries, university students have turned the serenade into an art form for hire.

I: What exactly do you do?

PS: Well, usually I am hired by men to sing love songs to women. Occasionally I am asked to sing to men, but only very exceptionally.

6 I: Can you explain it a bit more?

PS: The service is really a form of intimate *alfresco* theatre with love songs which are guaranteed to melt the hardest hearts. I usually wear a white tie and tails and sing amorous Italian songs. I carry chocolate hearts or flowers and when there is no balcony available I sing from trees or fire escapes!

I: How much do you charge for a serenade?

PS: It depends on whether a musician comes along or not. The basic rate is £450 but it can cost a lot more especially if I take a gondola and group of musicians along. Each serenade is different. The idea is to personalise them as much as possible.

I: How do people react?

PS: That's difficult to say because you never get the same reaction twice. Some people are so moved that they burst into tears. It's all very emotional.

I: Do you ever react badly? Do you ever get

used as an unwanted messenger?

PS: That is a major worry. We try to find out as much as we can about our clients to avoid unpleasant situations. You have to be very careful these days because a serenade can be completely misinterpreted. Once I was even accused of harassment and the woman called the police. Another time a neighbour called the police to complain about the noise. We really have to be extremely careful and discreet.

7 I: How long have you been a tree-climber, Mr Saw?

Mr S: I have been a tree surgeon and qualified tree-climber for the last 30 years.

I: How did you start?

Mr S: I was encouraged to climb trees for the Parks department when I left school at 14, because I was then quite small – only five feet, in fact – and not afraid of heights. It was really a natural progression from the things me and my mates got up to out of school.

I: Did you have any formal training?

Mr S: Oh yes. I went to Merristwood College in Surrey. I followed a course on tree care and tree-climbing and I learnt the basics of tree-climbing there – techniques like how to throw a rope over the branches of a tree, climb up it and get into a harness, that sort of thing.

I: What sort of things are you asked to do?

Mr S: Well, the work is extremely varied – anything from rescuing cats to conducting surgery on the tree.

I: What is the most exciting job you have done?

Mr S: Well, last year I was contacted by Jersey Zoo. They were conducting a bat conservation programme and this involved research work in the Comoros Islands. Apparently they had been forced to abandon the project once because they couldn't actually catch any of the fruit bats, which live at the top of fig trees. So they called me in for advice on tree-climbing and I ended up going on the trip. Catching a fruit bat up a tree isn't easy, but it was a great experience. Unfortunately, it's not the sort of thing you do every day.

I: Have you ever fallen out of a tree?

Mr S: Never. Although I've tackled trees over 100 feet high. Mind you, I wouldn't be around to talk to you if I had made a habit of falling!

I: Do you still climb trees?

Mr S: Very rarely. I'm a bit too old for climbing about in trees now. I have a job lecturing on tree-climbing at a horticultural college. Of course, if I was asked to return to the Comoros, I'd go like a shot. That's the sort of opportunity I couldn't miss.

Unit 6 Food and eating habits, Section A Listening

2 W: John, sorry to disturb you, but I was wondering if you know of a good restaurant around here. I've got some old friends staying with me at the moment, and they want to take me out to dinner. I've no idea where to go.

J: Well, let me think.

W: You know, somewhere with good food, pleasant, relaxed atmosphere that sort of thing.

J: The trouble is there isn't a great deal of choice in town. I mean if you want to take the car, then you've got some great restaurants not far away in the country ...

W: Well, we'd prefer to stay in town.

J: Well, one of the nicest restaurants I've been to is Gilbey's which is in the town centre.

W: Oh yes, I've driven past it. It's near the Town Hall, isn't it?

J: That's right. It's expensive but it's very refined and classy, you know, quite sophisticated food, and a great atmosphere but I don't know if it's open every evening.

W: Well, maybe we'll try that. I'd better give them a ring to find out if they're open.

J: But what about Indian food?

W: Oh yes, I love Indian.

J: Well, how about the Golden Bengal?

W: Oh, that's a great place, I spent an evening there with Jan and Phil - you know them, don't you?

J: Yes, I do.

W: I thought the food was OK, and the staff are very friendly. It was a bit noisy though, I suppose it was because it was a Saturday night. But it's worth going back to, I quite liked it.

J: What about Gino's? I went there to celebrate

my promotion last year. The wine was really excellent.

W: Yeah, I've been there, but I didn't rate the food much. It was a bit disappointing. I mean, the helpings were enormous, but my lasagne was cold and the service was a bit slow. It's one of those cliché Italian restaurants where the waiter comes round with an enormous pepper mill and grins at you.

5 JM: Hello, is that the Tourist Office?

TO: That's right. Can I help you?

JM: Yes, this is Jenny Maltravers from Maltravers Tours in Chiswick. We do guided tours and study seminars, and we're planning a visit to Bath with a group of people.

TO: OK, yes.

JM: What I need is the name of a good restaurant for us to have dinner at, around seven-thirty before we head on to Bristol.

TO: Right. What size group are we talking about?

JM: Well, fifty are booked at the moment, but it might grow to sixty.

TO: So about sixty people. Well, there are a couple I can recommend, there's the Walnut Tree but that's about five kilometres from the centre, and the Europa Hotel, which is very central but has less charm, you know it's one of those big hotels.

JM: Does the Walnut Tree have a separate room for large groups?

TO: No, but the Europa Hotel does.

JM: And what would be the price for a three-course evening meal?

TO: Well, at the Walnut Tree, it'll be fifteen pounds per person. The Europa is cheaper at ten pounds per head, but wine isn't included.

JM: And what's the cooking like?

TO: Well, the Walnut Tree is known for its innovative cooking, the chef is David Little, the brother of Alistair …

JM: Never heard of him …

TO: And the Europa is very nice too, very refined.

JM: Is there a vegetarian menu?

TO: Oh, yes there is. There's usually a vegetarian menu these days.

JM: Anything else you can tell me about them?

TO: Well, the Walnut Tree is a three star restaurant now, and the Europa is a two star.

JM: OK, well thanks for your help. I'll get back in touch if I need … Oh, can you give me their phone numbers?

TO: Yes, just hold on, I'll see if I can …

Unit 7 Expressing your opinions, Section A Listening

2 Interview 1

I: Excuse me. I'm doing a survey on the recent modernisation of this airport. Would you mind answering some questions?

A: Well, if you're quick.

I: Right um could you tell me um where you're going and why you're going there.

A: Yes, I'm flying to Barcelona on business.

I: Right. And and what about? Can you tell me how often you use the airport?

A: Yes, I use this airport approximately twice a month because of my work.

I: Right. And um what about, what do you think of the new restaurant?

A: I'm sorry, but I think it's tacky – cheap, vulgar, I mean – plastic cups, wobbly chairs, we deserve something better.

I: Right. Um. Okay. Right, now what about the speed of airport procedures and formalities?

A: Well, that varies. Now, some days they're all right, they can cope but on busy days they can't cope at all – if it gets overcrowded they just don't seem to have the staff to deal with the situation and there are delays.

I: Right, thank you. Um. What about the new parking facilities?

A: In my opinion the parking is too far from the terminals. I know there's a courtesy bus but it isn't frequent enough.

I: Right, er, and what about the transport links to the airport?

A: Transport facilities, public transport is pretty good. I think there are frequent rail services and buses, yes I think it's pretty good.

I: Okay. And the new signposting in the airport, what do you think of that?

A: Well I think it's deplorable. I mean, fortunately I'm used to the airport so I know where I'm going but if I were new to the airport I would not be able to find a single thing.

I: Thank you.

A: Thank you.

Interview 2

I: Excuse me.

B: Yes.

I: I'm doing a survey on the recent modernisation of this airport.

B: Oh right.

I: Would you answer some questions please?

B: Yes, yes, certainly.

I: Right, um. Could you tell me where you're travelling to please?

B: At this moment in time I'm going to visit my family in Budapest.

I: Oh right. Um and can you tell me how often you use the airport?

B: Um. Well, I go there twice a year.

I: Right. Umm. Now what do you think about the new restaurant?

B: Well, if you're here for a short while you'd choose fast food because you don't want to hang around and you've got to get served very quickly, so, as I've only had fast food here I didn't go for the other things in the menu, I think it was pretty good. Acceptable.

I: Good, thank you. Now what about the speed of the airport procedures and formalities?

B: Oh. It's very slow, I mean it's full of hold-ups, isn't it. One thing you're into another and then security and you're out of there and I find it all like giraffes in the zoo or something, it's very slow.

I: Right. Thank you. Um, now what about the new parking facilities?

B: That's very good, it's very convenient, you can get in, everything's marked and you know which section you're in but it you have to pay for all that of course, it's very expensive, I think.

I: Yes, okay. Um. The transport link to the airport. What do you think about that?

B: Well, I came by car so I don't really know.

I: Okay. And then what about the new signposting in the airport?

B: New signposting! It's as bad as it's ever been. Oh, I've been going round in circles. You follow a sign and you find that the arrow's pointing the other way.

I: Right. Thank you.

Interview 3

I: Excuse me. I'm doing a survey on the recent modernisation of the airport. Would you mind answering a few questions?

C: No, not at all.

I: Right. First, could you tell me where you're going?

C: I'm going to Istanbul on holiday.

I: Right. Thank you. Um and could you tell me how often you use the airport?

C: Well this is my first time. This is the first time I've flown so I'm rather excited but a little bit nervous.

I: Right. Yes. Um, what's your opinion of the new restaurant?

C: Yes, I tried that earlier. It's it's expensive and I didn't think there was a lot of choice, but the quality was quite good.

I: Okay. Um. What about the speed of airport procedures and formalities?

C: What, do you mean the check-in and things? (yeah) Um well, I thought they were very good actually, yeah, in fact I think my case was a little bit heavy but the guy was very friendly and sort of, you know kind of, and took it on, and I took a while to get all my documents out but they were, yeah, very patient, very friendly, yeah.

I: Good. Right. Um what about the new parking facilities?

C: I don't know anything about that because I came by train. But that was on time and very good and convenient. The you know the platform was very near the this concourse.

I: Right. So you would say that the transport links to the airport are pretty good then?

C: Yeah. Terrific.

I: Right. Okay. And what about the new signposting in the airport?

C: Well, it seems fine; I had to find the loo. Very soon. No I haven't got lost yet.

I: Thank you.

C: Okay.

4 Extract 1

A: Excuse me, we're doing some research. Have you got a moment?

B: Sure.

A: We're finding out about childcare facilities in this area, and I was wondering if you would answer some questions.

B: Well, I suppose so, but I'm not sure I can help very much. I don't have any children, you see, and I don't like them very much, actually.

Extract 2

C: Can you give an indication as to which way you're going to vote, sir?

D: I thought it was a secret ballot in this country.

C: Yes, but …

D: I thought that constitutionally I had the right not only to vote but also not to reveal how I voted to every Tom, Dick and Harry who asks me. Am I right or am I right?

C: You're right, sir.

D: I disapprove of this kind of survey anyway.

Extract 3

E: Is that Mr Jenkins?

F: Yes.

E: I was just ringing to give you my congratulations, Mr Jenkins.

F: What for?

E: You've won a fabulous two week holiday in St Lucia.

F: What? You're kidding!

E: No, I'm not. This is Grove and Hill Travel Agents, and you've won our first prize in this month's travel competition.

F: That's amazing.

E: So you'd like to accept the prize?

F: Well, of course I would.

E: Well, if you'd like to accept, then there are just a few questions to answer about our travel agency.

F: Hang on. I thought you said I'd won?

E: You will have as soon as you've answered these questions.

F: What kind of questions?

E: Just a few questions about the service our travel agency can give and how we can improve it.

F: No, I'm sorry but you've set me up, haven't you? This is a trick isn't it, some kind of advertising stunt. No, I'm sorry, but I'm not going to … I can't …

E: Oh all right, have it your own way …

Extract 4

G: Excuse me, can I ask you some questions about the government?

H: What do you mean?

G: Can I read you this statement and ask if you agree or disagree?

H: What are you on about?

G: This government has been in power for too long and should be replaced at the earliest opportunity. Do you agree, disagree or have

no opinion?

H: Oh, go away you silly little man. Go on, go away. I can't stand this sort of questionnaire.

Extract 5

I: And how do you feel about the soaps?

J: Soap operas! I love them. I watch them all. I've just finished watching EastEnders.

I: Oh really? So what happened this week then?

J: Is this part of the survey?

I: Well no. But I like EastEnders too and I'd be watching it as well if I didn't have to do this …

Unit 8 Leadership, Section A Listening

2 I: The subject of our programme this afternoon is Leadership. We have in the studio Graham Henshaw who is a historian and has recently published a book on the great Leaders of our Times.

Mr H: Hello.

I: Mr Henshaw. Perhaps you can tell us what, in your view, makes a really great leader?

Mr H: Well, to start with, I think we can learn a lot from history by studying the great men and women who've left their mark at different times – for both good and bad, I hasten to add. But, of course, many of the great leaders of the past were military chiefs, and depending on whose side you found yourself on, they were either national heroes or, er, dreaded tyrants. Take Genghis Khan, for example, he was undoubtedly an outstanding warrior and military leader, if you happened to be one of his followers, that is. But if you were unlucky enough to live in a country he plundered, you were more likely to see him as a dangerous madman. So you see, not everyone is likely to see these so-called great leaders in the same light.

4 I: But were all the great leaders of the past military chiefs?

Mr H: Oh no, of course there were also the great spiritual leaders who have changed the world. Men like Luther and Gandhi. But I think it is true to say that most people, even today, continue to identify great leadership with military models. I mean, just consider the criticisms our politicians get fired at them. How often do we hear them being compared unfavourably to wartime heroes such as Churchill or de Gaulle? Even though the job at hand is very different. What good would military strategy be for dealing with unemployment? I'm pretty sure it would be of little use. So even though these models no longer bear any relation to the complex workings of the modern world, we still measure ministers or company directors against them.

5 I: Can we say that there are some characteristics which all great leaders have in common?

Mr H: I think it is true to say that all successful leaders share a number of basic characteristics. For a start, they know exactly what they want to achieve, I mean, they have very clear objectives. Secondly, they never lose sight of their objectives and work towards them no matter what obstacles they may come up against. In this respect, they display great powers of concentration. The third common characteristic of great leaders is that they tend to believe that the end justifies the means. Of course, you can easily see the danger here. What is the difference between the madman and the truly great leader? I think the difference lies in the fourth characteristic. Great leadership should express the will of the people and improve their lot. It doesn't just serve personal ambition. In other words it has to be for the common good. Take Gandhi, for instance, he may have unleashed destructive forces, but his main purpose of freeing India was undeniably the popular will. Finally, I think we have to add success to our list. To be considered great, the leader has to be successful. I can't think of many examples of unsuccessful great leaders!

8 **Extract 1**
He has extraordinary leadership powers. A people person, he has great listening skills and is very decisive. He is somebody you can brief in great detail, who will brilliantly synthesise the points you've made and elaborate them. But above all he has a wonderful sense of humour which rubs off on everyone here at the museum and helps create a pleasant working atmosphere. And when the atmosphere is good, problems just seem to resolve themselves.

Extract 2
He was a deeply intelligent, mild-mannered and caring man, he had a tremendous capacity for inspiring confidence in everybody around him. I remember being very surprised to find such a person in uniform. He was admired and respected by all his men. He had one of the most important qualities in any leader: courage. I don't just mean physical courage, which you need of course as a soldier, but intellectual courage, without which all the other attributes of leadership amount to nothing.

Extract 3
I've had several managers in my career. Only one was excellent at his job. He knew exactly what the job entailed. He was a strong disciplinarian and above all extremely decisive – there were no grey areas: it was black or it was white, right or wrong. As a player that was what I found the most helpful – to know exactly where you stood.

Extract 4
She is the leader who has inspired me most in the many years I've worked in broadcasting. She's in charge of programmes, a difficult and demanding position which she manages with great skill. She has a great many qualities essential to the television world: enthusiasm, a willingness to delegate, and a sense of humour. I'll add the ability to have a wild idea and the courage to go with it, even if it runs against all the objectives. But I think, what I admire her for most, is her clarity of purpose and her ability to communicate it clearly to others.

Extract 5
I have worked under her at the agency for two years now and admire her immensely. She started out in sales and only went into advertising quite late in life. I suppose it was this start to her career that helps her understand the sort of problems faced by staff. Her particular quality is her innate antipathy to anything unpleasant. No one ever hears her say anything nasty about anyone. Without saying anything she sets a standard in

her behaviour so that people feel uncomfortable behaving badly, inadequately or inefficiently.

Unit 9 Environmental hazards, Section A Listening

2 PS: There's a chance that the heavy seas will break up the oil, which is described as light crude, but it will be an anxious three or four days before we know the extent of the damage to wildlife and to the coastline of what was, until now, some of the most unspoilt countryside in Britain.

I: Thank you, Peter. Peter Snell, reporting from the Hebrides. We'll bring you more news as we get it. So with the news of yet another oil-tanker disaster, this time much closer to home, I asked John Henderson, a Lloyds insurance broker, why these catastrophes keep happening, despite the modern equipment that is available to tankers today.

JH: Well, the point is that the majority of ships are not that new at all. In fact, the average age of tankers these days is over 13 years old, and the average age is getting older.

I: Why is that?

JH: Well, a large number of ships were built in the boom years of the seventies. But the decline in oil supplies meant that new ships weren't needed and the older ships were not replaced.

I: So one cause is that the ships are too old.

JH: Yes, that's right. Remember the *Aegean Sea*, for example, which was over twenty years old, which is really quite old for such a large ship.

I: Remind us of the damage the *Aegean Sea* caused.

JH: Well, it went down in 1992 off the coast of north-west Spain, and lost 70,000 tonnes of oil in one of Spain's richest fishing grounds.

I: But was it the age of the tanker which was the cause of the sinking?

JH: Strictly speaking, no. It was caused by human error, when the ship ran aground. But it was made worse because the age of the ship meant that the situation couldn't be retrieved.

I: So the age of the ship and human error are two causes of these catastrophes. Can't the risk of human error be avoided by the ship's equipment?

JH: You would think so, wouldn't you? But even a modern, well-equipped ship like the *Exxon Valdez*, which went down in 1988, ran aground because of human error.

I: This was in Alaska, wasn't it?

JH: That's right, Alaska in 1988.

I: Any other causes?

JH: A third cause of course is the weather. It can be extremely dangerous in a storm, and these huge tankers are at the mercy of the waves. For example, it was the heavy seas that caused the fate of the *Katina P* in April 1992.

I: Where was that?

JH: Off the coast of Mozambique.

I: And how old was the *Katina P*?

JH: Twenty-six years old.

I: So even older than the *Aegean Sea*?

JH: That's right. As I said, the age of the ship seems still to be one of the main causes for these disasters. Only the year before the *Katina P* went down, a 22 year old ship, called the *Kirki* was lost off the coast of Australia.

I: So what's being done about it?

JH: Well, there is legislation being brought in, and there's a chance that the older ships will have been phased out by the early twenty-first century.

I: But until then … ?

JH: Until then, this may not be the last of the disasters.

I: John Henderson, thank you for joining us.

JH: Thank you.

5 Extract 1
We're very aware of the hardship that the loss of our client's tanker will cause you individually and the community as a whole, which is why I have come here to reassure you that the liability is covered by the shipowners' policy and all your claims for compensation will be met by my company.

Extract 2
You cannot believe the damage the oil has caused out there. I went to sea this morning, and there's nothing but dying seals and dead fish. It'll take years for the sea to restock itself, and it's not just my livelihood which has been wiped out. It's going to affect everyone around here, from shopkeepers to hotel owners. It's an absolute disaster.

Extract 3

We're very aware that the situation is critical and in the short term we are devoting both resources and finance to clean up the beaches and to support the local community. In the long term, we intend to introduce legislation which will lead to tighter controls on chartering older ships and banning those which do not meet the safety requirements from entering British waters. But the immediate concern is to bring relief to the community as quickly as possible.

Extract 4

Every time this sort of disaster occurs, the response from the government is always the same – legislation will be brought in to do this, every effort will be made to do that – but nothing happens at all. The seas around here will be polluted and the wildlife destroyed for the next ten years. My party has been campaigning for the last two years for a ban on tankers entering these waters if they are older than fifteen years, but no one takes any notice until it happens again … and again and again.

Extract 5

We are of course co-operating with the authorities and we will be organising an official enquiry into the disaster, but our initial reports suggest that human error was not an element in the loss of the ship, nor did the age of the ship have any bearing on the matter. It is likely that the weather conditions contributed significantly to the situation in which control was lost and the tanker was driven onto the rocks.

Unit 10 Conscription, Section A Listening

3 I: There has been no compulsory national service in Britain now for decades and many people would like to see this situation changed. Some say that it is character-forming and helps develop a feeling of national pride and identity. Others say that rather than military service, some sort of compulsory civilian service – helping the elderly or other such social work – would be both useful to society as a whole and formative for young people. We thought it would be interesting to find out how other countries deal with national service and so

we have invited Tessa Davis …

TD: Hello.

I: Hello. … who has recently completed a comprehensive report on National Service in Europe, to tell us what happens elsewhere.

TD: Well, the situation varies enormously from one country to another. The country with the longest military service is Greece where all able-bodied young males have to serve a minimum of 19 months in the army. Then, at the bottom of the scale you have Austria with six months and Portugal with only four. Apart from the UK, only Ireland and Luxembourg have none at all.

I: Is there any chance that the countries in the European Union will standardise their national service laws?

TD: Well, although many countries are changing their laws and the length of service – there is a general tendency to shorten the service – there is no move towards bringing all the national service laws in line or having a single European model.

I: What about alternative national services?

TD: In some countries there is no choice. Greece, for example. Not even people opposing the use of arms on religious grounds can avoid doing their time in the military. Spain is another example – although there are plans to change this situation and conscientious objectors may already, very exceptionally, work for the Red Cross. And then, on the other hand, you have countries like Holland and Sweden where large numbers of young people opt for civilian service.

I: Which country has the most demanding national service?

TD: Switzerland, where although the laws are perhaps the most demanding it is also where they are the least resented. There, every able-bodied male must do three weeks' training every year until the age of 32. This is in addition to the 17-day initial training session which they do when they reach the age of 20. There's also an alternative civilian service for those who object on religious grounds.

I: So there are quite a few variations to the idea of national service?

TD: Yes, well, as you can see, there are as many solutions as there are countries. But I think it is true to say that there is a general softening of these laws and fewer people do their service today in each individual country than, say, 15 years ago.

5 **Extract A**

I: Why do you think conscription is so important?

A: I think it's an important part of your formative years. After all, your country has given you maybe ten years of education, and now it's time for you to do something for your country in return. I think there are many things to be said in its favour. Perhaps most important is that it gives you a chance to get to know people. For many people it's the only opportunity they will ever have to mix with all sorts of different people. I think it has an important social aspect to it. Conscription ensures there is a close interaction between the army and society.

I: Some people claim that a professional army would be more efficient.

A: It might be more efficient but with conscription you can use manpower and not high technology with massive staff costs to run the armed services. A totally professional army is much more expensive to run than a conscripted army.

I: But surely there are some jobs in the armed forces which require a high degree of training and skill.

A: Yes, of course, but those jobs can be left to the professionals. There are lots of military jobs which require very little training, such as driving jeeps or carrying guns and conscripts can do them very well. Leave the tricky jobs to the professionals and let the conscripts do the dirty work. Above all, I think it's important to serve one's country and it gives you a real sense of national identity.

Extract B

B: It's such a waste of time, though. I mean a year away from real life. I think it's particularly tough on those people who are studying for a higher degree and who have to interrupt their studies to do their military service. When you interrupt your studies to do something non-intellectual for a long time, it makes it difficult to start again.

I: But surely doing your military service is a way of giving something back to the system which has supported you and educated you.

B: But it's such a waste of time and effort, misguided effort I call it. We don't need an army these days anyway. There must be better ways of paying one's debt to society. It's the trivial aspect of the army which I can't understand, the idea of discipline for its own sake, even if it's at the expense of efficiency. It doesn't matter if the tanks don't work, as long as the men have neat uniforms and shiny boots. It really is so petty and such a waste of time.

Extract C

C: I do think that some form of service is a good idea but as I'm a pacifist, I'm against military service. How about some form of public service, such as working in a hospital or helping old people or something like that? I think a few months of compulsory civilian service would be a very good idea. I'd certainly be happy to do something like that, but definitely not in the armed forces.

Unit 11 Time matters, Section A Listening

3 **Extract 1**

Well, I'm married, with a small child. I chose to work nights because the shifts are longer which means fewer days at work in the week. And it's better paid because the hours are unsocial, even though I have much less to do because the patients are all fast asleep. I only do it for the money because of house payments. But it's exhausting and extremely disruptive. I'm lucky to have my mother living near the hospital, because she helps out with the child minding. Now I'm expecting another child and I'll probably go on to part-time day shifts. It's impossible to have a proper family life when I'm on nights, and it strains the relationship. I'm much too tired to go out on the days I'm not on duty. Fortunately, my husband's a doctor, so he understands the problem. But even though he works at the same hospital, his timetable rarely coincides with mine, and we sometimes go for a week without seeing each other.

Extract 2

I chose to work at night because I'm a loner and a night bird. I really enjoy the city at night, because there's no traffic, and much less stress than during the day. You meet some fairly unusual customers at night as well, which makes it a bit more interesting. I'm married but the kids are grown up and live away from home. My wife found it tough at first but she's adapted and has her own life with girlfriends. Because I'm a loner it hasn't really affected my social life. I mean, I don't like going out in the evenings. My main pleasure is fishing on some lonely stretch of river on a day off. I'm my own boss when I'm at work. My cab is like a second home for me. I can sleep any time so I have no problems catching up. Not when I'm driving of course!

5 **Extract 1**
I remember the first time I flew from England to Japan. We left at about midday and had lunch above the North Sea. Then at about half past three in the afternoon, it started to get dark much earlier than usual of course. By the time we had dinner it was in the middle of the night, and we finally landed in the morning Japanese time, but according to our body clocks, it was just about time to go to bed. Well, I was tired, of course for a few hours, but they say you should try and keep going until the time you're meant to go to bed, which would have meant staying awake for about thirty hours or so. In the middle of the afternoon, I was feeling physically sick with jet lag. It really is a strange experience. I slept well that night, but I didn't really recover until about two days later. You wake up at strange times in the night as well for a few days after the flight.

Extract 2
It's so disruptive, putting the clocks forward. It's supposed to conserve energy, but I really don't see how that works. It's one of those typical bureaucratic decisions which irritates everybody. The worst time is in March when you suddenly find yourself getting up in the dark again – just when you'd got used to the light spring mornings. And the children take ages to adapt. You try telling a three-year-old that she's got to eat an hour later or go to bed an hour earlier! When they get back from school they're irritable and miserable. It takes about a week before they adapt to the new times. It's all very annoying.

7 RP: On the 27th of March Europe sets its clocks forward one hour. It's a ritual act greeted with general approval: the extra hour of daylight in the evening gives the illusion of a

longer day, our leisure time expands and we relax. Doctor Petersen, is changing the clocks simply an opportunity to spend time in the light with our friends?

DP: Well, the changes are more than social. They are biological as well. You see, human biological patterns follow a twenty-four hour cycle, like the geophysical pattern of the sun and the moon and the tides, and these are adapted to the alternation of day and night and light and darkness. We have a sleep-wake cycle regulated by the daily rotation of the earth around its axis, and these so-called circadian rhythms operate at every level of our organs and cells. They govern heart rate, body temperature, respiration patterns, levels of stress, sleep hormones and blood coagulation.

RP: What happens when these biological rhythms are disturbed?

DP: Disturbance occurs when our internal clocks and our environment mismatch, which happens not only when the clocks change but when crossing time zones and doing shift work. The consequences of this disturbance range from digestive and sleep problems to cardiac disorders. It can also affect behaviour, metabolism, mood and performance. Blood flow, for example, varies around the clock, and doctors now know that the blood clots more easily in the early morning, adding to the risk of heart attacks or strokes.

RP: Is there any medical help to rectify the problem of disturbed biorhythms?

DP: Soon there will be drugs to correct disturbed biological rhythms.

RP: Are there any positive effects in the change of biorhythms?

DP: Oh, absolutely. It can be helpful in the timing of surgical intervention and radiotherapy and can also be used in preventative medicine. Our metabolism and therefore our absorption and elimination of drugs varies considerably over 24 hours. So, in theory, treatment can be timed so that the desired effects of taking certain drugs will reach their peak at the right biological time.

RP: I see. Now, are the effects of putting the clocks forward in the spring different from putting them back in the autumn?

DP: Well, it's clear that daylight plays an important role in our lives. We feel happier and more energetic on longer, brighter days. But our inner rhythms are also a result of social, physical, nutritional and genetic factors. From the north to the south of Europe or the USA, there are big differences in daylight, length of the working day, timing and constitution of meals, sleep time, temperature and total amount of sunshine. All these factors can contribute to a change of biorhythms, and in turn contribute towards our wellbeing and our capacity to work efficiently or to enjoy ourselves.

RP: So manipulating biorhythms by changing the clocks can have important economic as well as social and biological effects?

DP: Exactly.

Unit 12 Town and country, Section A Listening

4 To: Good morning, can I help you?

W: Yes, good morning, I've just got a few queries, I wonder if you can help me sort them out.

To: I'll see what I can do.

W: Can you tell me when Sudeley Castle is open?

To: Yes, of course, Sudeley castle, Sudeley, I think it's open all day, someone asked me this a week or so ago.

W: I hope so, we want to go there this morning.

To: Here we are, I've got the guide, yes, it's open from 11 in the morning until 5 in the afternoon, well not quite all day, but morning and afternoon.

W: Eleven am to five pm, OK, that's great. Er, can you tell me how much it costs to get in?

To: Yes, it costs £4.50 for adults and £3 for children. It sounds a bit expensive but there's a lot to do there. I think it's worth the money.

W: So £4.50 for adults and £3 for children. No, that's about what you pay in most of these places, I suppose. OK, now, another question: what exactly is Snowshill Manor? What can you see there?

To: Oh, it's a museum, an absolutely fascinating collection of all sorts of things, like clocks and masks, and cabinets, and there's a whole room full of Samurai armour.

W: Samurai? Well, the kids will like that. Do you pay to get into this museum?

To: Yes, you do, I think it's about three pounds fifty.

W: Is it open this time of year?

To: Yes, it's open until the end of September, so there are a few weeks before it closes.

W: Right, we'll try it. One last thing. My husband wants a weekend break at some point and someone has recommended the Lygon Arms, but I've forgotten where it is. Is it somewhere suitable for touring the region?

To: Yes, it certainly is. It's in Broadway, which is on the edge of the Cotswolds. It's a lovely old hotel, about four hundred years' old and you sleep in huge beds.

W: How much does it cost?

To: I've got the brochure here somewhere. Yes, they're offering weekend breaks at £210 per person for the whole weekend.

W: £210! That sounds a bit expensive.

To: Well, that includes breakfast and dinner, and the food is meant to be out of this world. So there are no extra costs.

W: None at all? Well, that makes it much more attractive. Well, I think I'll give them a ring to see if they've got a room for next weekend. Have you got their number?

To: Yes, I've got it right here. Here it is, it's 01386 8522 double 5.

W: Hang on I haven't got anything to write it down with. Oh, here we are. OK, what was the number again?

To: 01386.

W: 01386 … yes.

To: That's the code for Broadway. 8522 double 5.

W: 8522 double 5. OK, yes, I've got it 01386 8522 double 5. Good, well, thank you very much.

To: Enjoy your visit. Good-bye.

5 To: Good morning, madam. Can I help you?

W: Yes, I'd like some information about the Cotswolds. I gather they're some place around here, and I'd like to have a look around.

To: Well, you've come to the right place, because we're right in the centre of the Cotswolds.

W: Well wouldn't you know it? Do you hear that, honey?

M: I sure did.

W: We're right in the heart of the Cotswolds. That's just great.

To: Do you have a map?

M: Yes, we do, right here.

W: That's no good, you got us lost already. No, we don't.

To: Here we are, compliments of the Cotswolds Tourist Authority. Now, let me see, we're here in Stow.

W: Can you see that, honey? Make sure you get a good look at it.

M: I can see it, I can see it.

To: Now, if you'd like me to suggest some places to visit ...

W: We sure would, wouldn't we?

To: Well the most beautiful place I think in the Cotswolds is Bibury.

W: Bibury, Bibury ...

To: It's right here on the A433 between Burford and Cirencester, just south of here. Can you see it?

M: You mean Bibury.

To: Well, we pronounce it Bibury. Anyway, it's a very pretty little village on the River Coln, well worth seeing. There's a good hotel there called the Swan Inn, and you should see the row of cottages called Arlington Row.

W: Right.

To: Another pretty village, well more of a small town is up here, called Chipping Camden.

M: Nice name.

To: The high street in Chipping Camden is very beautiful ...

W: Is that two words?

To: That's right madam, C-H-I-double-P-I-N-G C-A-M-D-E-N.

W: I got it. OK. Where else?

To: Northleach is very pretty as well, it's a small wool town with a famous church.

M: Where's this Northleach place?

To: It's on this road, the A429 from Stow to Cirencester. About twenty minutes away. Then, I'd go and take a look at Burford, just on the edge of the Cotswolds, here we are, Burford, just off the A40. It's also got a splendid high street, and there are lots of tea shops and gift shops and things like that.

W: Sounds great.

M: No more major purchases, honey, we agreed.

To: Then here in Winchcombe, can you see, just north-east of Cheltenham on the B4632, is Sudeley Castle, with some wonderful gardens.

W: Sudeley Castle, OK, I got it. Great we'll try it out.

To: If you like old buildings, have a look round Snowshill Manor over here just north-east of Sudeley and south-west of Chipping Camden, can you see?

W: OK. Snowshill, I can see.

To: And as far as other things to see and do, well, there's a model railway, here in Bourton-on-the-Water, yes, that's just here.

M: A model railway, hey, that sounds great.

W: Please excuse my husband, he's got the brain of a five-year old.

To: Well, I expect you'd also be interested in the Wildlife Park here just south of Burford on the A361.

W: Wildlife Park?

To: Yes, it's a kind of zoo, full of tigers and monkeys and rhinos and other wildlife. And then there's a country park here just outside Broadway. There we are, Broadway Tower Country Park.

W: What's there to do in this country park?

To: It's got things for children to do, but it's also got a fascinating tower to climb and you get this fabulous view of the Cotswolds and even into Wales.

W: Anything else?

To: Well, my favourite is the Farm Museum, just outside Witney.

W: Farm museum?

To: Yes, it's an old farm with lots of farm animals, and exhibitions. It might be a very good place to start, so that you get an idea of Cotswold life. It's a very traditional part of the country.

M: Sounds like one great big theme park.

W: Excuse my husband, I'm just going to take him to that farm museum ... and leave him there.

To: Glad to be of service. Good-bye.

Answer key

Unit 1 Foundation unit, Section A

1 The people listening to the presentation are future examiners.

The following information given by the organiser probably helped you make up your mind: *when you're running the exam, you don't have to keep stopping the tape to give the candidates time to complete their answers.*

The questions about procedure at the end of the recording probably also helped you identify the people as future examiners: *How long should we allow candidates for completing the answer sheet at the end the exam? Should we intervene at all during the exam? For instance, to repeat certain instructions if some candidates look puzzled?*

2 1 length of exam   2 question types   3 text sources   4 number of sections   5 number of items   6 number of times each text is heard   7 text types   8 skills tested   9 instructions

3

Listening	Text type	Number of times text is heard	Text length
Section A	Monologue	2	
Section B	Short descriptive passage	1	
Section C	Dialogue or discussion	2	
Section D	Series of short extracts	2	Each extract lasts about 10-30 seconds

4 The topic is the CAE exam. Extracts 1, 2, 3 and 5 are about this topic. The speakers have English, French and American accents. The exam candidate in Extract 3 is French and the passenger in Extract 4 is American.

5

Extract	Number of speakers	Setting	Role of speakers	Attitude of speakers
1	1	Instructions for Paper 4 Listening	Examiner	Matter of fact, neutral
2	1	Instructions for Paper 4 Listening	Examiner	Matter of fact, neutral
3	2	After sitting Paper 4 Listening	A candidate talking to someone she is familiar with	The candidate is upset; the other person is sympathetic
4	2	At the airport check-in	Passenger, airline check-in assistant	The passenger is angry and impolite; the assistant is conciliatory and calm
5	2	After Paper 4 Listening	Two examiners	Relaxed, informal

Unit 1 Foundation unit, Section B

1 1 Three people participate in the conversation; they are a CAE examiner and two exam candidates. The examiner does not know the candidates. The candidates know each other, they have been together in the same class. Their names are Patrick and Alessandro, Alessandro speaks the most.

2 Four different topics are covered: personal information about Patrick; how Patrick is in the class; personal information about Alessandro; how Alessandro spends his free time.

3 The examiner is responsible for changing topic.

4 The examiner changes topic by asking the candidates questions. First he says to Alessandro *Can you tell us something about how Patrick is in the class?* Then he says to Patrick *Could you tell us a little bit about Alessandro?* Finally he says to Patrick *Could you tell us a little bit about how Alessandro spends his spare time?*

5 The speakers take turns by taking the initiative and by asking and answering direct questions.

6 Patrick performs rather better than Alessandro.

2 1 true   2 true   3 true   4 true   5 false   6 true   7 false

3 Suggested answers;
Activities *d* and *h* provide the most practice in the skill of conveying information. Activities *b* and *f* are useful if they are used as models for candidates' own production. Activities *c* and *e* may help candidates organise their ideas. Activities *a* and *g* are perhaps the least useful.

4 Candidate A's description was restricted to a description of the room; the description was clear, however.
Candidate B included her own impressions, feelings and opinions in her interpretation of the scene.

5 Candidates have the opportunity to both speak individually and to interact together. They work with visuals, in this case, pictures which are similar but not exactly the same.

6 1 The topic is the kind of person represented by something in a visual.

2 The candidates conclude that the person is a representation of modern life. A potato in the visual could represent either an English or a German person. This person never leaves his chair: he eats junk food, which he orders by telephone, rather than cooks; he uses his remote control to watch TV and videos all the time. (Such a person is known in English as a 'couch potato'.)

3 No, they speak about the same amount.

4 They use the following expressions to show agreement: *yeah; yes – sure; yeah, yeah; But that's it; Yeah, that's true.* They also repeat part of what the other candidate has said. They use the following expressions to show disagreement: *No, it's not so obvious; I don't completely agree; I don't know.*

5 Patrick's arguments are the most convincing. He seems surer about what he wants to say.

7 Phase A: greetings; introducing yourself or others; talking about likes and dislikes
Phase B: describing objects or people; comparing and contrasting; interpreting a picture
Phase C: agreeing and disagreeing; interpreting a picture; expressing opinions; justifying opinions; persuading
You will need the other language functions (reporting decisions, explaining decisions and summarising) in Phase D.

8 accuracy b)   fluency c)   pronunciation d)   task achievement e)   interactive communication a)

9 Patrick performs rather better than Alessandro. He would probably get a mark of 7 whereas Alessandro might get 6.
Morena seems to be a little bit more accurate and fluent than Samantha. In this part of the test, she might get a mark of 6 whereas Samantha might get one of 5.

Unit 2 Different backgrounds, Section A

3 Speaker 1: Sharon Harper comes from Canada and she now lives in Finland.
Speaker 2: Stephen Wareham comes from Britain and he now lives in Hungary.
Speaker 1 answers the following questions in this

order: 1, 2, 6, 5, 4, 6, 7, 3.
Speaker 2 answers the following questions in this
order: 1, 7, 6, 3.

4 Speaker 1:
1 for a summer job
2 nine years
3 family and friends, hot Canadian summers, hot
  weather, autumn colours
4 the physical appearance of the country – the
  rocks and woods
5 the cultures – Finland has a strong sense of
  history whereas America is a new country; the
  Finns are more outward looking than North
  Americans who are egocentric
6 saunas, simple pastimes, genuineness of the
  people
7 lack of social charm – bluntness, long dark
  winters.

Speaker 2:
1 Hungarian wife
3 Sunday newspapers, pubs, seaside
6 Hungarian character, sense of humour, quality
  of life – low crime rate, cultural life, public
  transport;
7 negative outlook, lack of initiative,
  bureaucracy, air pollution

6 1 ✔ 2 x 3 x 4 ✔ 5 x 6 ✔ 7 ✔ 8 x

7 1 A 2 C 3 D 4 C 5 A 6 C 7 A

Unit 3 Unusual homes, Section A

2

	Interview 1	Interview 2	Interview 3
Home	Windmill	Houseboat	Converted railway carriage
Advantages	Peaceful and beautiful	Cheap to buy, feeling of space, no close neighbours, change scenery, sense of freedom	Space outside, not a dangerous place for the children
Disadvantages	Draughty, damp, lack of space, two hundred yards down a dyke	No disadvantages mentioned	Unpleasant surroundings, frightening, isolated, feeling of insecurity, cold and draughty, far from the town centre
Reason for choice of home	Husband was enthusiastic about restoring it, cheap to buy	Couldn't afford a decent house, the boat was relatively cheap to buy	Couldn't afford a decent house or flat

4 Speaker 1:
1 very damp
2 thought it was very small
3 15 years
4 created dining and kitchen area, washing machine area and bedroom
5 on a dyke in Holland near Rotterdam

Speaker 2:
1 good condition
2 suited his taste
3 –
4 very little; did some decorating
5 in the city

Speaker 3:
1 cold and draughty
2 found the area grim and frightening
3 two years
4 a little decorating, made curtains
5 in a railway siding

Speaker 2 doesn't answer question 3.

5 Speaker 1 e)   Speaker 2 d)   Speaker 3 c)

6 1 living in   2 cedar tree
3 tree surgeon   4 a shed or outbuilding
5 only £500 or very little
6 workshop   7 nature   8 high or strong winds
9 damaged   10 its growth
11 local authorities   12 planning permission

Unit 3 Unusual homes, Section B

1 Suggested answers:
Positive meanings: at<u>trac</u>tive, <u>char</u>ming, (<u>sol</u>id), <u>struc</u>turally sound
Negative meanings: au<u>stere</u>, <u>dan</u>gerous, <u>de</u>relict, (<u>fall</u>ing down), <u>hid</u>eous, run-down, se<u>vere</u>-<u>look</u>ing, <u>ug</u>ly
Similar meanings: attractive, charming; austere, severe-looking; dangerous, <u>un</u>safe; de<u>mol</u>ish, pull down; derelict, falling down, <u>ru</u>in; do up, im<u>prove</u>, <u>ren</u>ovate, re<u>store</u>; <u>ma</u>sonry <u>prop</u>erty

Unit 4 Communicating, Section A

3 Speaker 1 c)   Speaker 2 e)   Speaker 3 a)
Speaker 4 d)   Speaker 5 b)

4 1 elderly person: letter writing
2 parent: intercom   3 business person: fax
4 disabled person: cordless phone
5 teenager: telephone

5 1 x   2 ✔   3 x   4 ✔   5 ✔   6 ✔   7 ✔   8 x

6 Task 1: 1 F   2 D   3 C   4 A   5 H
Task 2: 6 G   7 F   8 E   9 B   10 A

Unit 5 Unusual occupations, Section A

1 Suggested answers:
1 professional tree-climber: branches, conservation, heights, horticulture, park, rope, safety harness, tropical
2 serenader: balcony, garden, gondola, heart, love, opera, passion, repertoire, roses, style, tenor, voice
3 lock-keeper: bank, canal, conservation, cottage, fishing, flooding, navigation, river
The following words are unsuitable for describing any of the jobs: aroma, Chanel, cosmetics, create, fragrance, *nez*, Paris, perfume, scent

2 Suggested answers:
– **How long have you been a <u>lock</u>-<u>keeper</u>, Mr Fielder**?
– Oh dear, let me think – umm – I <u>started</u> when I was 2<u>5</u>, so that means I've been at it for uh <u>twenty</u>-<u>one</u> <u>years</u> now. Yeah, that's it – <u>three</u> <u>years</u> on the <u>Oxford</u> <u>canal</u> and the *past* <u>eighteen</u> <u>years</u> <u>here</u> on the <u>Reading</u> <u>stretch</u>. <u>Twenty</u>-<u>one</u> <u>years</u> in all.
– **<u>What</u> did you do <u>before</u> you became a <u>lock</u>-keeper?**
– I used to be an <u>electrician</u>. That's what I <u>trained</u> as.
– **Do you ever <u>regret</u> <u>leaving</u> your <u>profession</u>?**
– <u>Oh</u>, <u>no</u>. <u>Absolutely</u> <u>not</u>. Right from the <u>start</u> I <u>realised</u> this was the <u>one</u> <u>job</u> that I would <u>love</u> to <u>do</u>. And I was <u>right</u>.

– **When** is your **most** **busy** time of year?
– The <u>summer</u> months. I can easily work a <u>ten-hour</u> <u>day</u> with all the <u>holiday</u> <u>traffic</u> and the <u>upkeep</u> of the <u>flower</u> beds along the <u>side</u> of the lock.

3 – **Many people imagine life on the river as uneventful and easy-going. Is this right?**
– Yes, <u>people</u> often <u>ask</u> me if I ever get <u>bored</u> sitting around here! In fact, I <u>get</u> <u>up</u> at six most mornings, and even in <u>winter</u> when there are fewer <u>boats</u> about, there is a lot to do controlling the water <u>level</u>. When it <u>rains</u> hard in the <u>night</u>, I can be up half a dozen times attending to the weir <u>gates</u>. No, I'm afraid the popular image of the pipe-smoking old man, <u>leaning</u> against the lock gate, <u>waiting</u> for the occasional <u>boat</u> is far from the truth.

You probably found it difficult or even impossible to guess the missing words. This is because they are all words which convey lexical meaning

4 Suggested answers:
– I <u>believe</u> you are the <u>founder</u> of <u>Serenading</u> <u>Service</u> – is that <u>right</u>?
– <u>Yes</u>, that's right. I <u>started</u> the <u>service</u> <u>three</u> <u>years</u> <u>ago</u> when I <u>realised</u> that <u>British</u> <u>people</u> were <u>desperate</u> for <u>romance</u> with a <u>capital</u> 'R'. I thought there would be a <u>clientele</u> for a <u>hired</u> <u>serenader</u>.
– **How** did you <u>begin</u> your <u>career</u> as a <u>singer</u>?
– I <u>started</u> <u>singing</u> as a <u>choirboy</u> and at the age of <u>ten</u> I was chosen to sing alongside <u>Placido</u> <u>Domingo</u> at a <u>charity</u> do. That's what really got me <u>started</u> on a <u>musical</u> career. I went on to <u>study</u> <u>music</u> and then I <u>joined</u> an <u>Opera</u> <u>company</u>.

5 – **Where did the idea of serenading come from?**
– From <u>my</u> studies <u>of</u> Renaissance music, <u>and</u>, <u>of</u> course, opera, which is full <u>of</u> serenades. On the continent, especially <u>in</u> Spain <u>and</u> Italy where it still thrives, it is a traditional romantic experience. Over <u>the</u> centuries, university students <u>have</u> turned the serenade <u>into</u> <u>an</u> art form <u>for</u> hire.
– **What exactly do you do?**
– Well, usually I am hired <u>by</u> men <u>to</u> sing love songs <u>to</u> women. Occasionally I <u>am</u> asked <u>to</u> sing <u>to</u> men, but only <u>very</u> exceptionally.

All the missing words in this extract convey grammatical meaning and are therefore not

essential for an overall understanding of the meaning of the extract. You were probably able to understand the meaning of the extract without the words. You probably didn't find it very difficult to complete the gaps.

6 1 Love songs.
2 Balconies, trees, fire escapes.
3 The basic rate is £450 but it can cost a lot more.
4 Some people are so moved that they burst into tears.
5 They find out as much as they can beforehand about their clients.

7 1 thirty years   2 fourteen   3 (quite) small
4 of heights   5 care and tree   6 rescue a cat
7 surgery   8 zoo   9 fig tree   10 (fruit) bat
11 fallen   12 100 feet   13 tree-climbing

Unit 6 Food and eating habits, Section A

2

	Restaurant	Opinion	Comments
Man	Gilbey's	S	Refined, classy, sophisticated food, great atmosphere
	Golden Bengal	S	
	Gino's	S	Excellent wine
Woman	Gilbey's	N	No comment
	Golden Bengal	S	Food OK, friendly staff, noisy
	Gino's	D	Disappointing food, slow service

5 1 very central   2 yes   3 £15   4 £10   5 yes
6 innovative   7 refined   8 yes   9 yes
10 three star

Unit 6 Food and eating habits, Section B

1

Scores:

1 A 3	B 0	C 2	D 1
2 A 0	B 1	C 3	D 2
3 A 2	B 3	C 0	D 1
4 A 3	B 2	C 1	D 0
5 A 2	B 3	C 0	D 1
6 A 2	B 3	C 0	D 1
7 A 0	B 3	C 2	D 1

Food is: very important: 17–21
quite important 9–16
unimportant: 0–8

Unit 7 Expressing opinions, Section A

2

	Speaker 1	Speaker 2	Speaker 3
Destination	Barcelona	Budapest	Istanbul
Reason for travel	Business	Family reasons	Holiday
User frequency	Twice a month	Twice a year	First time
Refreshments	Tacky, cheap, vulgar plastic cups, wobbly chairs	Pretty good, acceptable	Expensive very little choice, quite good quality
Speed of formalities	Variable	Very slow	Nice, friendly people
Parking facilities	Too far from terminal	Convenient but expensive	No opinion
Transport to the airport	Pretty good	No opinions come-by car	Terrific, train is convenient
Signposting	Deplorable	Bad – totally lost going round in circles	Fine – hasn't got lost yet

Speaker 3 is the most positive. This is probably because the person is flying for the first time. Speaker 1 is the most critical and assertive. This is probably because this person travels very frequently out of necessity and flying is a means of transport which should be as convenient and comfortable as possible.

4 Task 1: 1 G   2 A   3 H   4 C   5 B
   Task 2: 6 C   7 A   8 F   9 E   10 D

Unit 7 Expressing your opinions, Section B

5 The photo was originally published in a newspaper. It shows Greenpeace demonstrators protesting in front of the British Prime Minister's residence at 10 Downing Street in London. They are protesting against a nuclear reprocessing plant in Sellafield, Cumbria, UK.

Unit 8 Leadership, Section A

1 1 Cleopatra   2 Martin Luther King
   3 Indira Gandhi   4 Mao Tse Tung
   5 Elizabeth I   6 De Gaulle   7 Gandhi
   8 John F. Kennedy   9 Genghis Khan
   10 Churchill

2 The speaker uses the following words:
   history, great, hero(es), tyrant(s), outstanding, warrior, follower(s), plunder(ed), dangerous, madman

3 Well, to start with, I think we can learn a lot from history by studying the great men and women who've left their mark at different times – for both good and bad, I hasten to add. But, of course, many of the great leaders of the past were military chiefs, and depending on whose side you found yourself on, they were either national heroes or, er, dreaded tyrants. Take Genghis Khan, for example, he was undoubtedly an outstanding warrior and military leader, if you happened to be one of his followers, that is. But if you were unlucky enough to live in one of the countries he plundered, you were more likely to see him as a dangerous madman. So you see, not everyone is likely to see these so-called great leaders in quite the same light.

4 – But were all the great leaders of the past military chiefs?
   – Oh no, of course there were also the great spiritual leaders who have changed the world. Men like Luther and Gandhi. But I think it is true to say that most people, even today,

continue to identify great leadership with military models I mean, just consider the criticisms our politicians get fired at them. How often do we hear them being compared unfavourably to wartime heroes such as Churchill or de Gaulle? Even though the job at hand is very different. What good would military strategy be for dealing with unemployment? I'm pretty sure it would be of little use. So even though these models no longer bear any relation to the complex workings of the modern world, we still measure ministers or company directors against them.

The speaker asks questions and then answers them himself: *How often do we hear them being compared unfavourably to wartime heroes such as Churchill or De Gaulle? What good would military strategy be for dealing with unemployment?*

5 1 c)   2 e)   3 b)   4 d)   5 a)

The speaker uses the following words and phrases to list the characteristics: *For a start, Secondly, The third common characteristic, I think the difference lies in the fourth characteristic, Finally.*

8 Task 1: 1 E   2 C   3 B   4 D   5 F
   Task 2: 6 F   7 B   8 C   9 D   10 H

Unit 8 Leadership, Section B

2 Suggested scores:
   1: (a) 0 (b) 1 (c) 2   5: (a) 1 (b) 0 (c) 2
   2: (a) 2 (b) 1 (c) 0   6: (a) 0 (b) 2 (c) 1
   3: (a) 2 (b) 1 (c) 0   7: (a) 0 (b) 1 (c) 2
   4: (a) 1 (b) 1 (c) 1   8: (a) 0 (b) 2 (c) 1

Your leadership potential:
12–17: you appear to have many of the characteristics of a leader
6–11: you are well on the way to influencing people
1–5: you show more signs of follower-ship than leadership

Unit 9 Environmental hazards, Section A

2 The causes of tanker disasters mentioned in the report are: 1 old ships, 2 human error, 3 the weather

3

Name	Date of Sinking	Age of Tanker	Location
Aegean Sea	1992	20 years old	NW Spain
Exxon Valdez	1988	Modern ship	Alaska
Katina P	1992	26 years old	Mozambique
Kirki	1991	22 years old	Australia

5 Task 1: 1 H 2 D 3 C 4 A 5 E
Task 2: 6 B 7 D 8 E 9 F 10 H

Unit 10 Conscription, Section A

3 1 Greece 2 19 months 3 Portugal
4 four months 5 UK, Ireland, Luxembourg
6 Greece, Spain 7 three weeks 8 32 years
9 17 days 10 20 years

4 The following statements express ideas in favour of conscription: 2, 4, 5, 6, 7

5 Speaker A: 2, 4, 5, 6, 7
Speaker B: 1, 3, 8
Speaker C does not make any of the statements. He is against military service but for a compulsory civilian service.

6 You could use the following words to describe the speakers:
Speaker 1: old-fashioned, enthusiastic, right-wing
Speaker 2: passionate, angry and left wing
Speaker 3: left-wing

7 Speaker 1 would probably agree with statements 1, 3 and 7.
Speaker 2 would probably agree with statements 2, 4, 5 and 6.
Speaker 3 would probably agree with statements 2 and 5.

Unit 10 Conscription, Section B

2 The following issues are mentioned in the article: 1, 2, 4, 6.

Unit 11 Time matters, Section A

3 Speaker 1 is a nurse. She has not adapted satisfactorily to night work.
Speaker 2 is a taxi driver. He has adapted satisfactorily to night work.

4 – Both speakers are married.
 – Speaker 1 chose to work at night because she is better paid; speaker 2 prefers working at night because it is less stressful, he enjoys being alone and likes the night.
 – Speaker 1 mentions fewer work days and better pay; speaker 2 finds driving less stressful at night and enjoys the unusual customers he meets.
 – Speaker 1 finds working at night exhausting, it means that she doesn't have a proper family life, it strains the relationship (with her husband); speaker 2 doesn't mention any disadvantages.
 – Speaker 1 would like to change job; Speaker 2 is satisfied with his working hours.
 – Speaker 1 says she is too tired to go out on the days she works at night; Speaker 2 says it doesn't affect his social life.

5 Speaker 1 is talking about jet lag.
Speaker 2 is talking about putting the clocks forward.

Speaker 1 felt sick but recovered after two days.
Speaker 2 says that his children were irritable and miserable and took a week to recover.

7 1 D 2 C 3 B 4 D 5 A 6 C

Unit 11 Time matters, Section B

3 1 E   2 C   3 A   4 –   5 B   6 F   7 –   8 D

5 The original sentences are:
Take time to work; it is the price of success.
Take time to think; it is the source of power.
Take time to play; it is the secret of perpetual youth.
Take time to read; it is the fountain of wisdom.
Take time to be friendly; it is the road to happiness.
Take time to love; it is the joy of life.
Take time to laugh; it is the music of the soul.

Unit 12 Town and country, Section A

4 1 11 am   2 5 pm   3 £4.50   4 £3   5 museum
6 end of September   7 Broadway
8 £210 per person   9 none   10 01386 852255

5 1 Bibury: a row of cottages
2 Chipping Camden: a beautiful high street
3 Northleach: a famous church
4 Burford: a splendid high street (tea and gift shops)
5 Sudeley Castle: wonderful gardens
6 Snowshill: old buildings
7 Bourton-on-the-water: a model railway
8 south of Burford on the A361: wildlife park
9 Broadway: a country park
10 Witney: farm museum